the Organist's Liturgical Year

o r g a n

Kevin
Mayhew

We hope you enjoy the music in this book.
Further copies of this and other books in the series are available
from your local music shop or Christian bookshop.

In case of difficulty, please contact the publisher direct by writing to:

The Sales Department
KEVIN MAYHEW LTD
Buxhall
Stowmarket
Suffolk IP14 3BW

Phone 01449 737978
Fax 01449 737834
E-mail info@kevinmayhewltd.com

Please ask for our complete catalogue of outstanding Church Music.

Front cover photograph courtesy of Images Colour Library, London.
Reproduced by kind permission.

Cover designed by Jaquetta Sergeant.

First published in Great Britain in 1998 by Kevin Mayhew Ltd.

© Copyright 1998 Kevin Mayhew Ltd.

ISBN 1 84003 207 3
ISMN M 57004 403 0
Catalogue No: 1400185

1 2 3 4 5 6 7 8 9

Music Editors: Nicola Caporali
Music setting by Christopher Ballam

Printed and bound in Great Britain

Contents

ADVENT ARIA

(after Christian Balle)

Adrian Vernon Fish

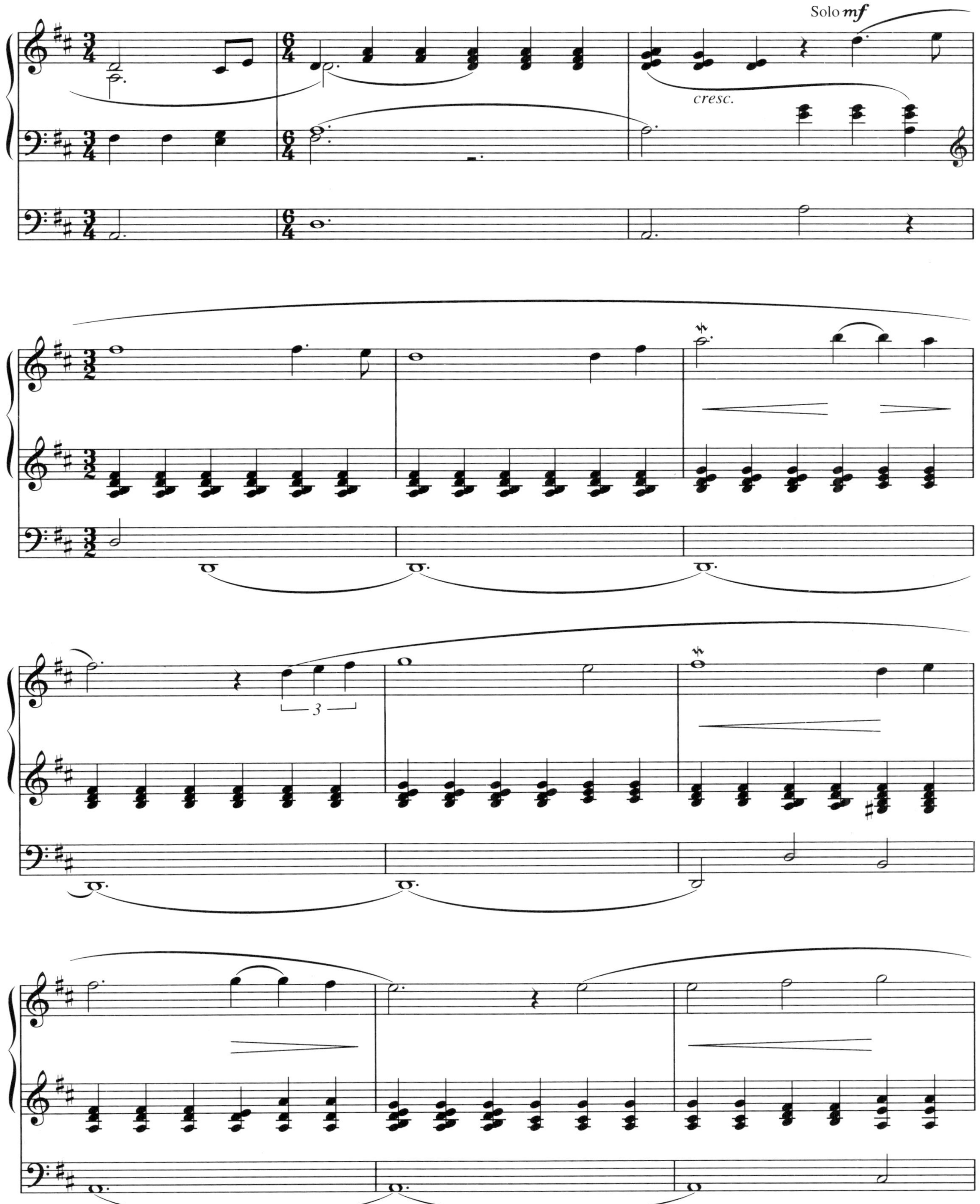
Solo mf
cresc.

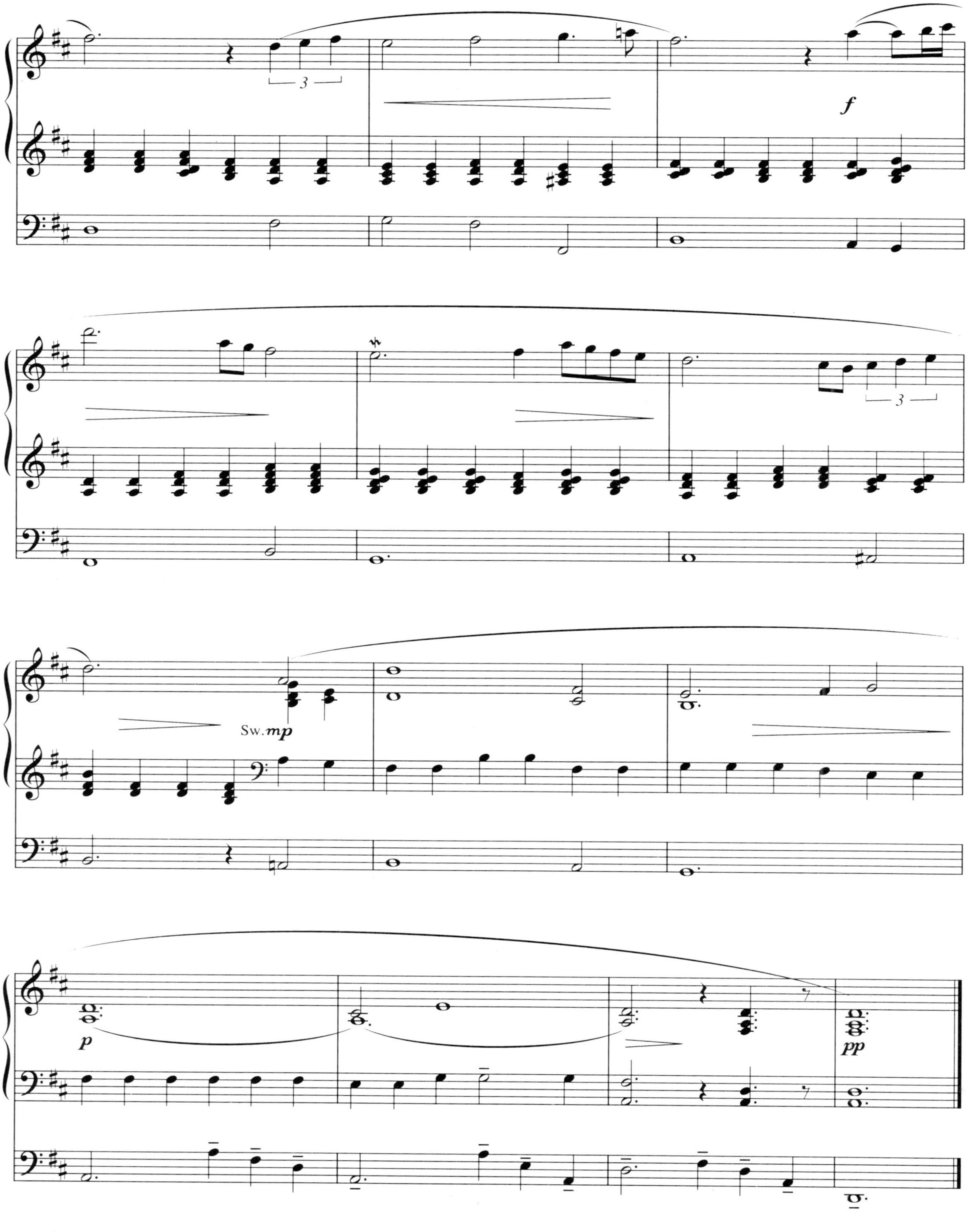
Sw.

MELISMATA VARIATIONS

Richard Proulx

Variation II
Sw. + 1⅗'

Variation III
Sw. + 4'

Variation IV
Soft Reed (or Princ. 8')

Ped.

ADVENT REFLECTIONS

Rosalie Bonighton

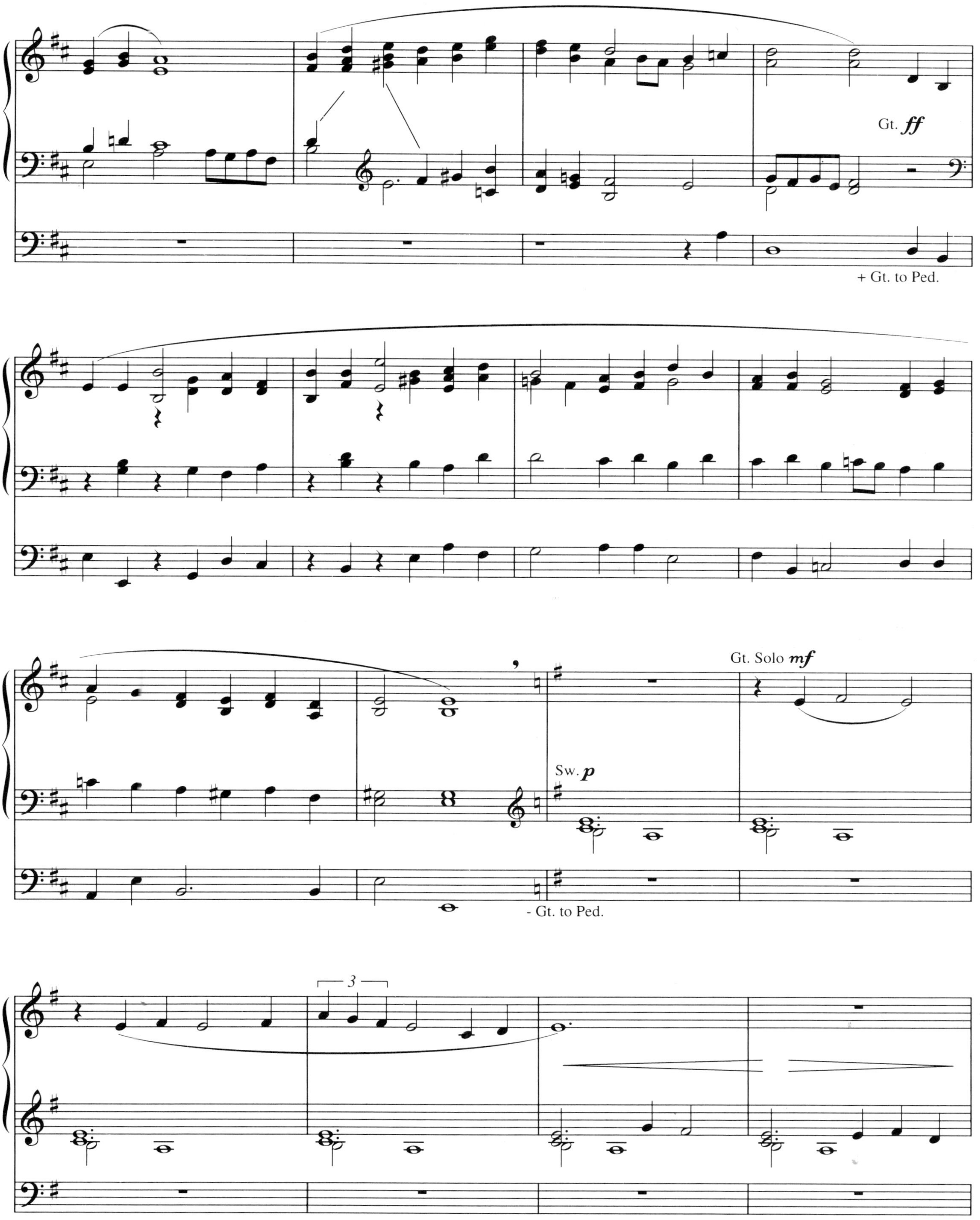
Gt. ff
+ Gt. to Ped.
Gt. Solo mf
Sw. p
- Gt. to Ped.
3

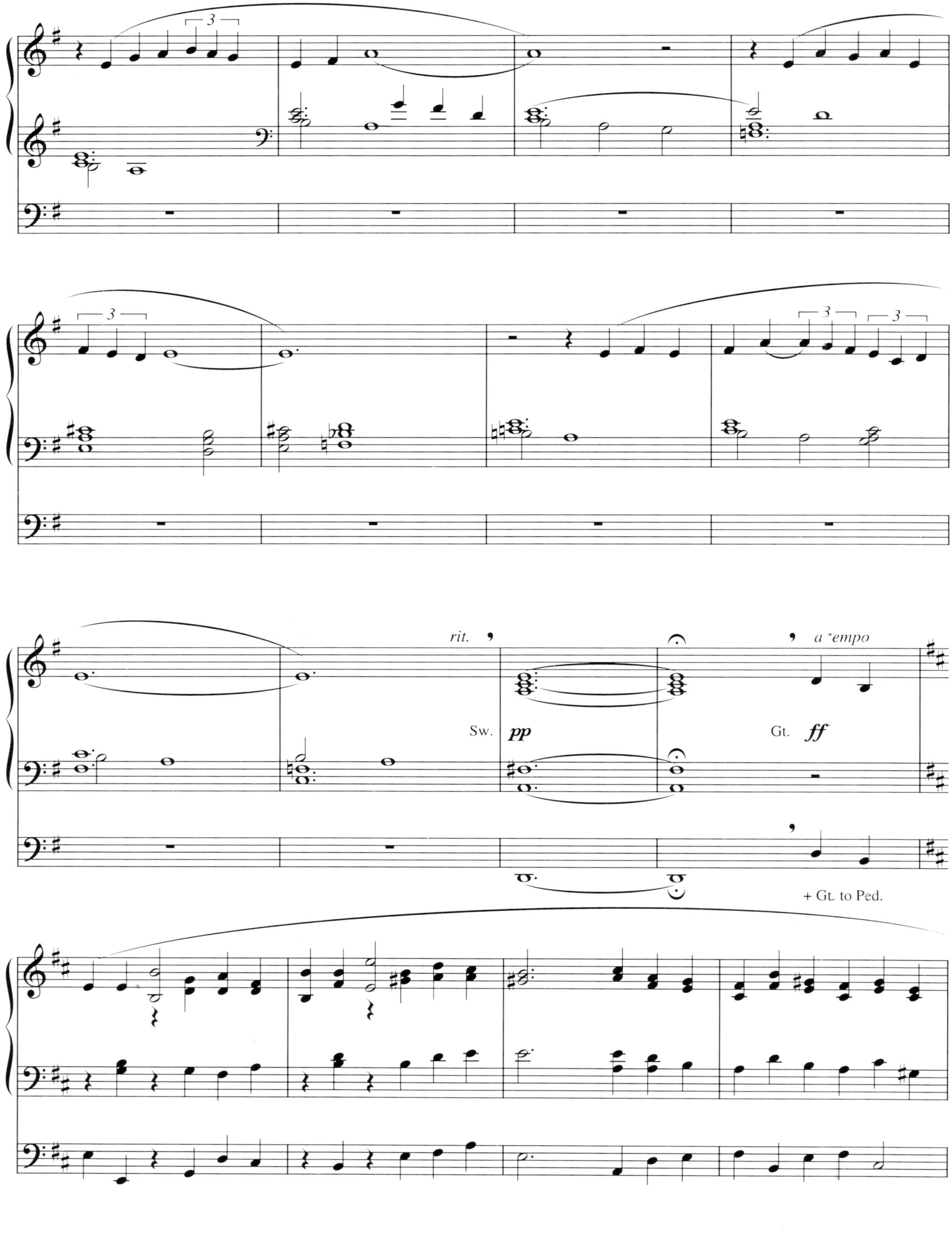

rit.
a tempo
Sw. pp
Gt. ff
+ Gt. to Ped.

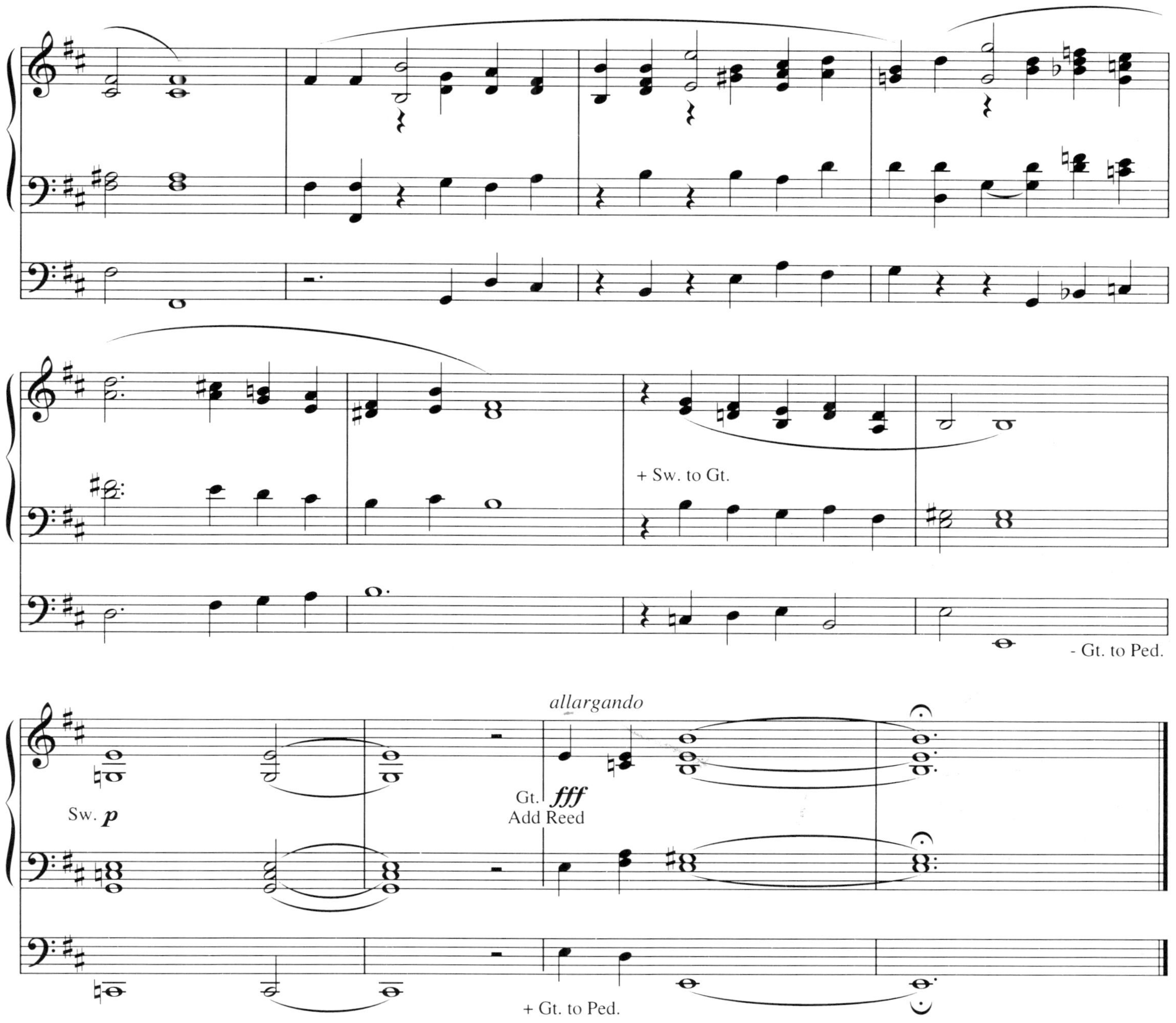
+ Sw. to Gt.
- Gt. to Ped.
allargando
Sw. p
Gt. fff
Add Reed
+ Gt. to Ped.

ARIA

Simon Clark

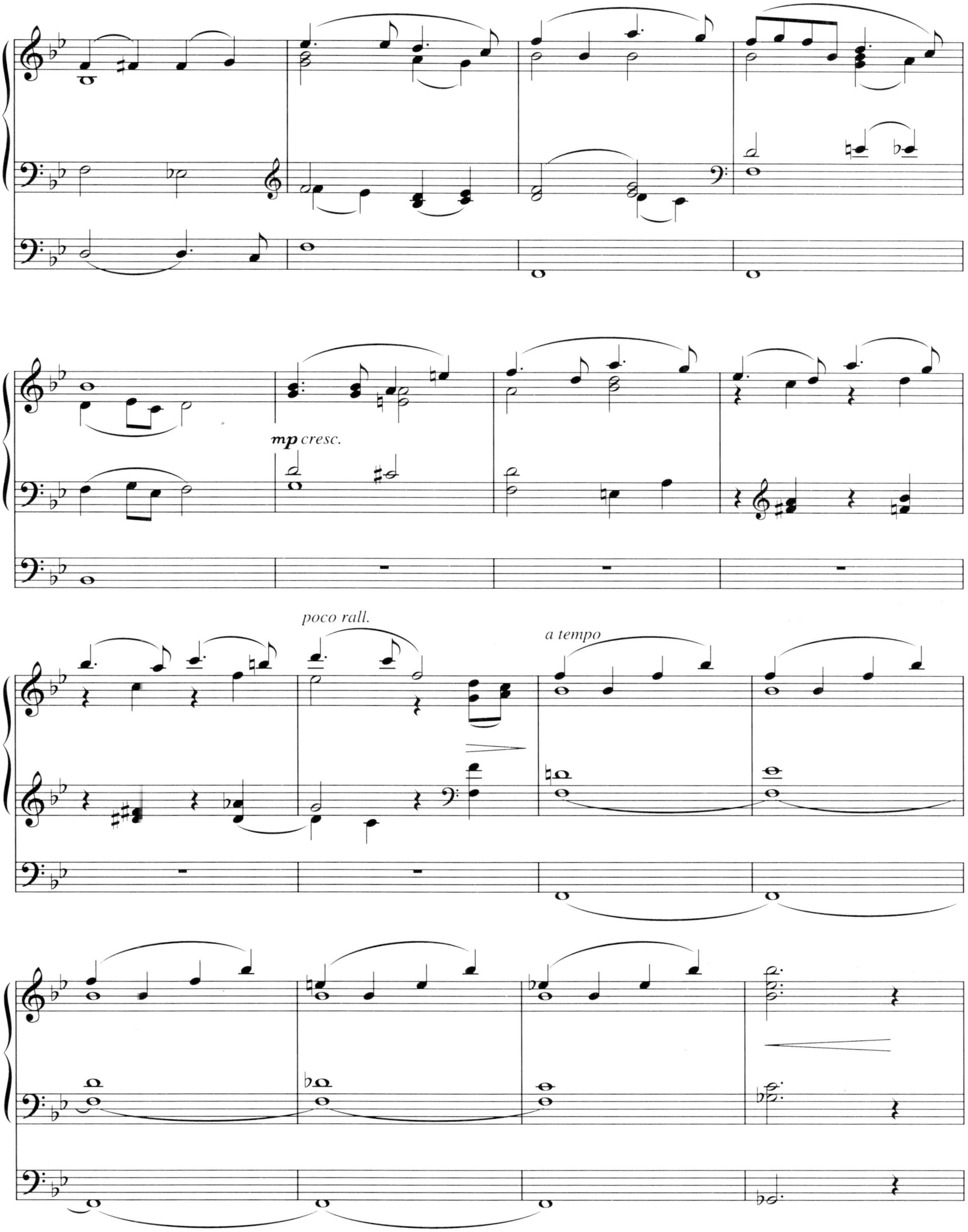
mp cresc.
poco rall.
a tempo

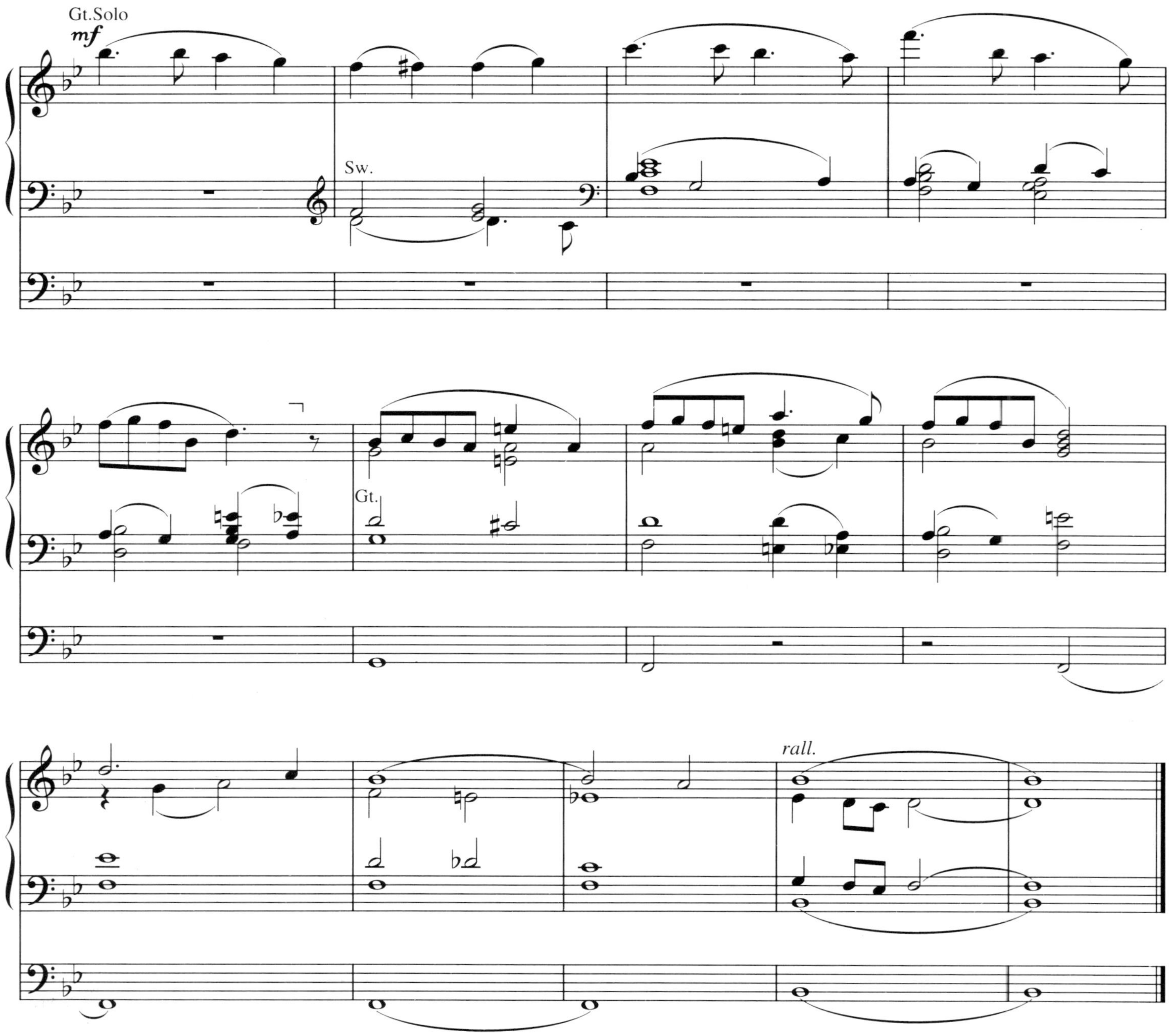
Gt.Solo
mf
Sw.
Gt.
rall.

PASTORALE

Richard Lloyd

Sw. Strings 8', 4'
Gt. Flute 8' + Sw to Gt.

Poco lento, senza rigore

poco rall.

Fine

a tempo

poco rall.

D.C. al Fine

ECHO CAROL

John Marsh

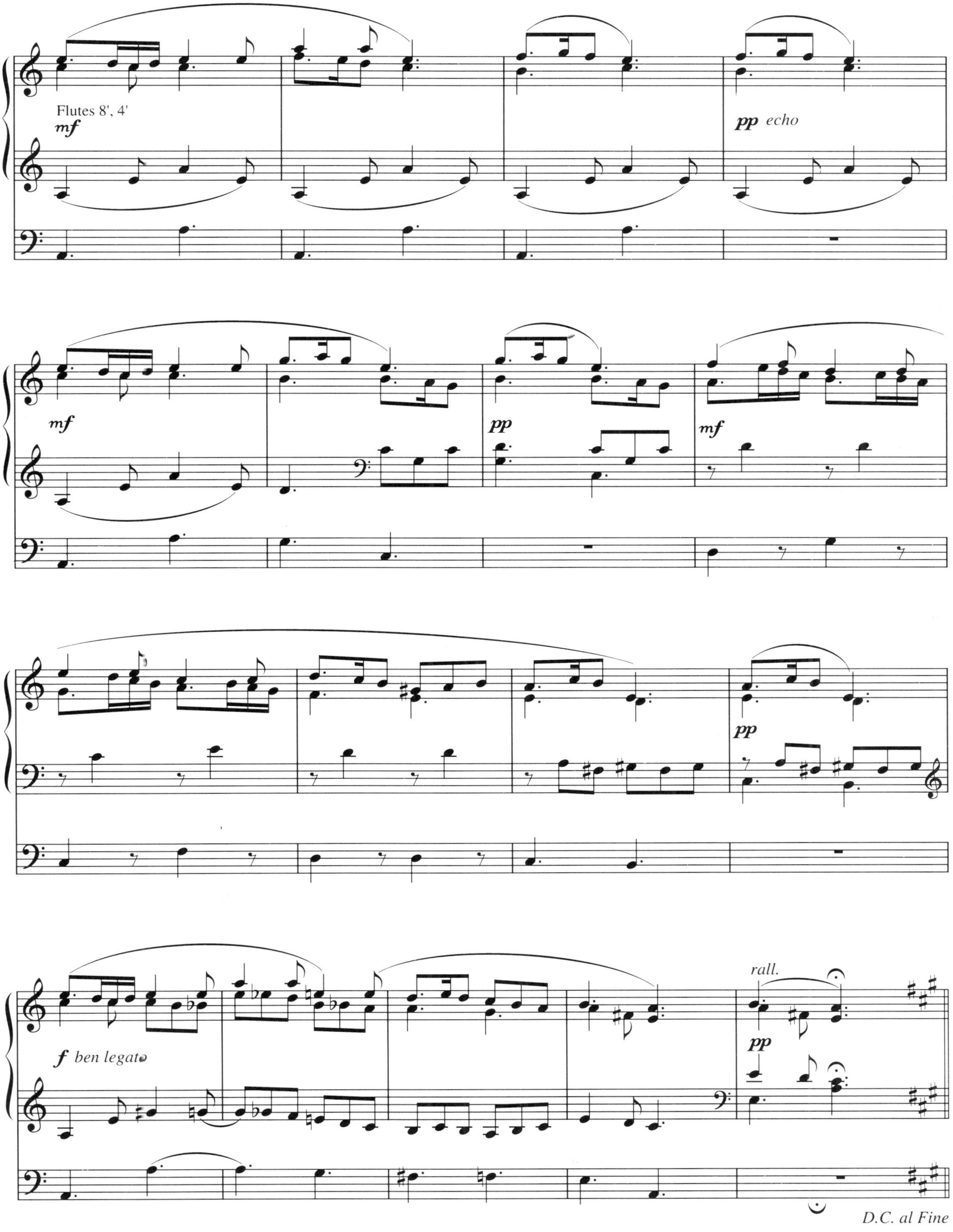

Flutes 8', 4'
mf
pp echo
mf
pp
mf
pp
f ben legato
rall.
pp
D.C. al Fine

BRING HIM GOLD, INCENSE AND MYRRH

Colin Mawby

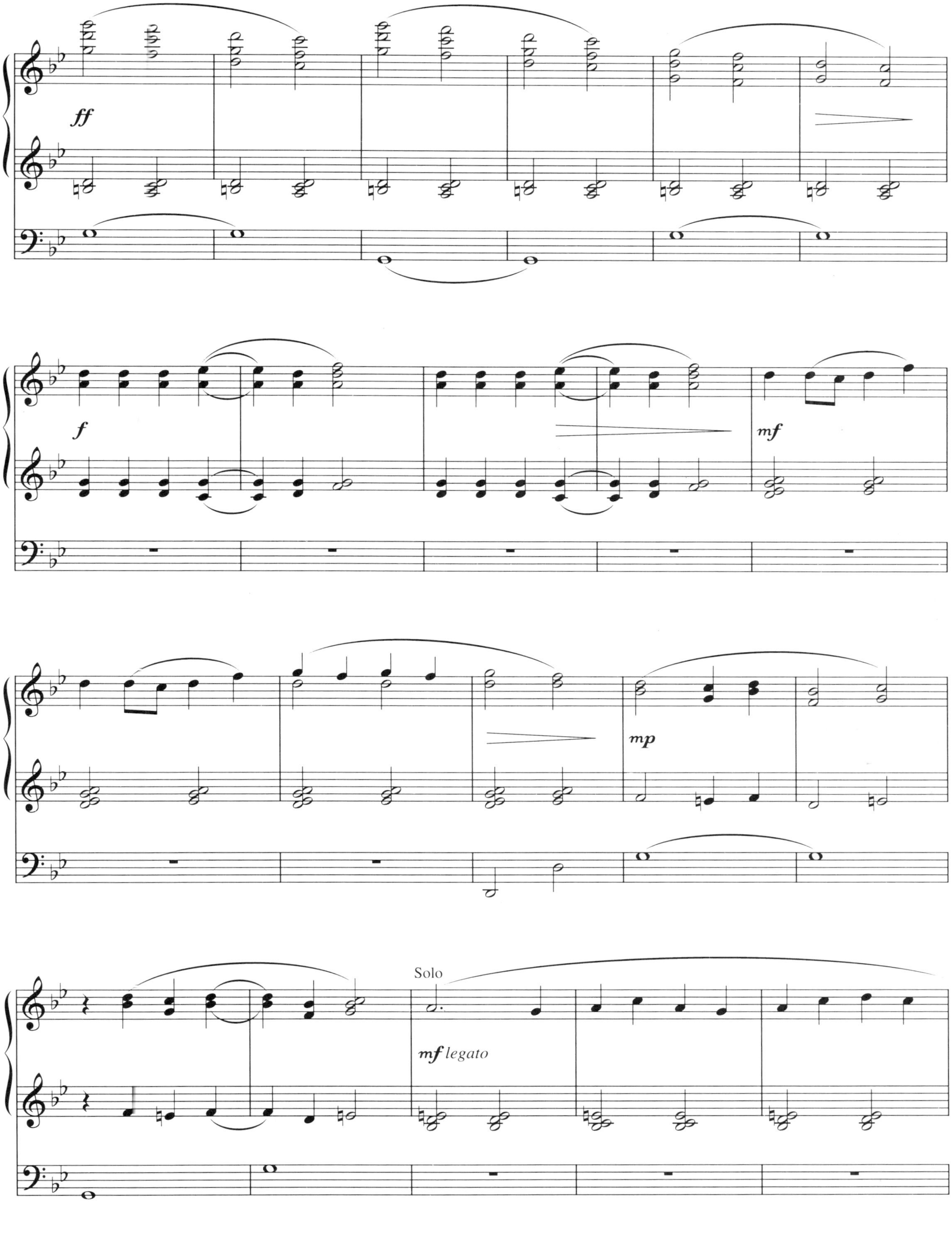
ff
f
mf
mp
Solo
mf legato

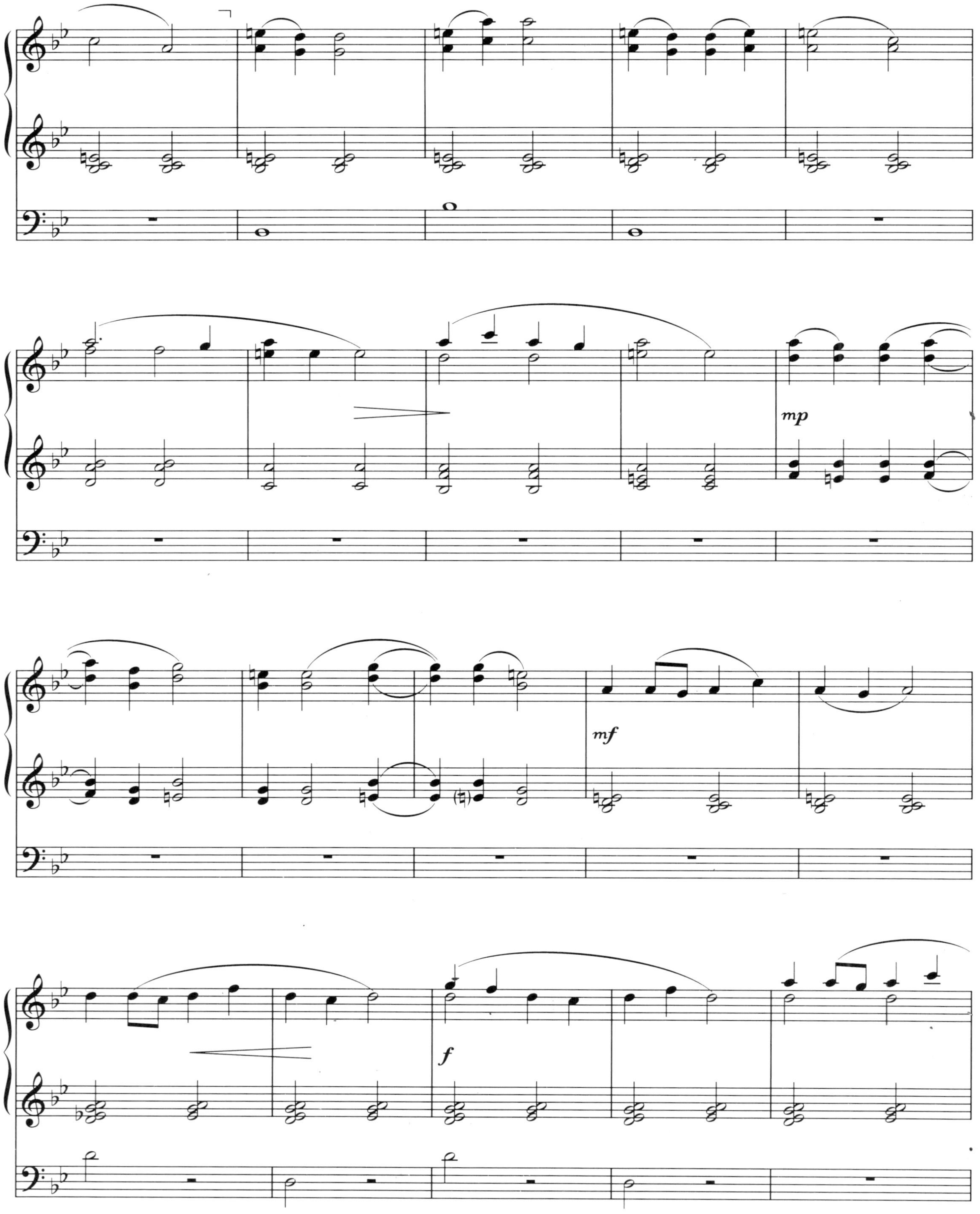
mp
mf
f

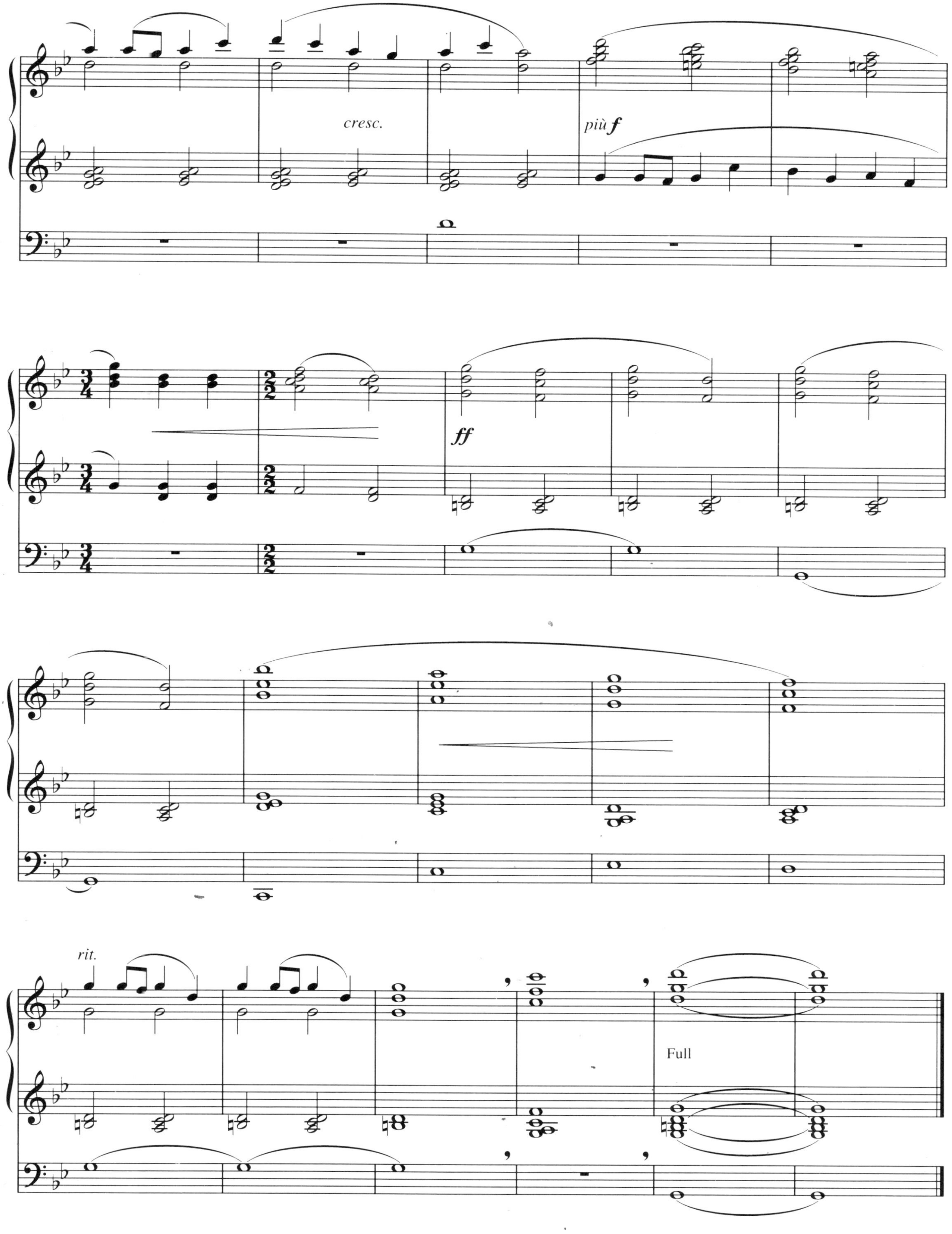
cresc.
più f
ff
rit.
Full

A CAROL

Andrew Fletcher

Andante pastorale, ma sempre con moto

poco rit.
a tempo
Solo, come prima
mp
f
p
Sw.
largamento
Gt. (+ Sw.)
meno mosso
Solo
Sw.
rall.
dim.
ppp

BAPTISM OF THE LORD

Malcolm McKelvey

Sw. Salicional, Celeste
Gt. Flute 8'
Ped. 16', 8' + Gt. to Ped.

Poco adagio
Sw. **pp**

cresc.
+ Sw. Reeds
ff
- Sw. Reeds
- Gt. 2'
- Gt. 4'
- Sw. to Gt.
rall.
Adagio
Sw. Sal.
Gt. Fl.
dim.
Gt. Dulc.
pp
rall.
Sw.
Ped. Dulc.

PAEAN ON THE MORNING
OF CHRIST'S NATIVITY

Andrew Gant

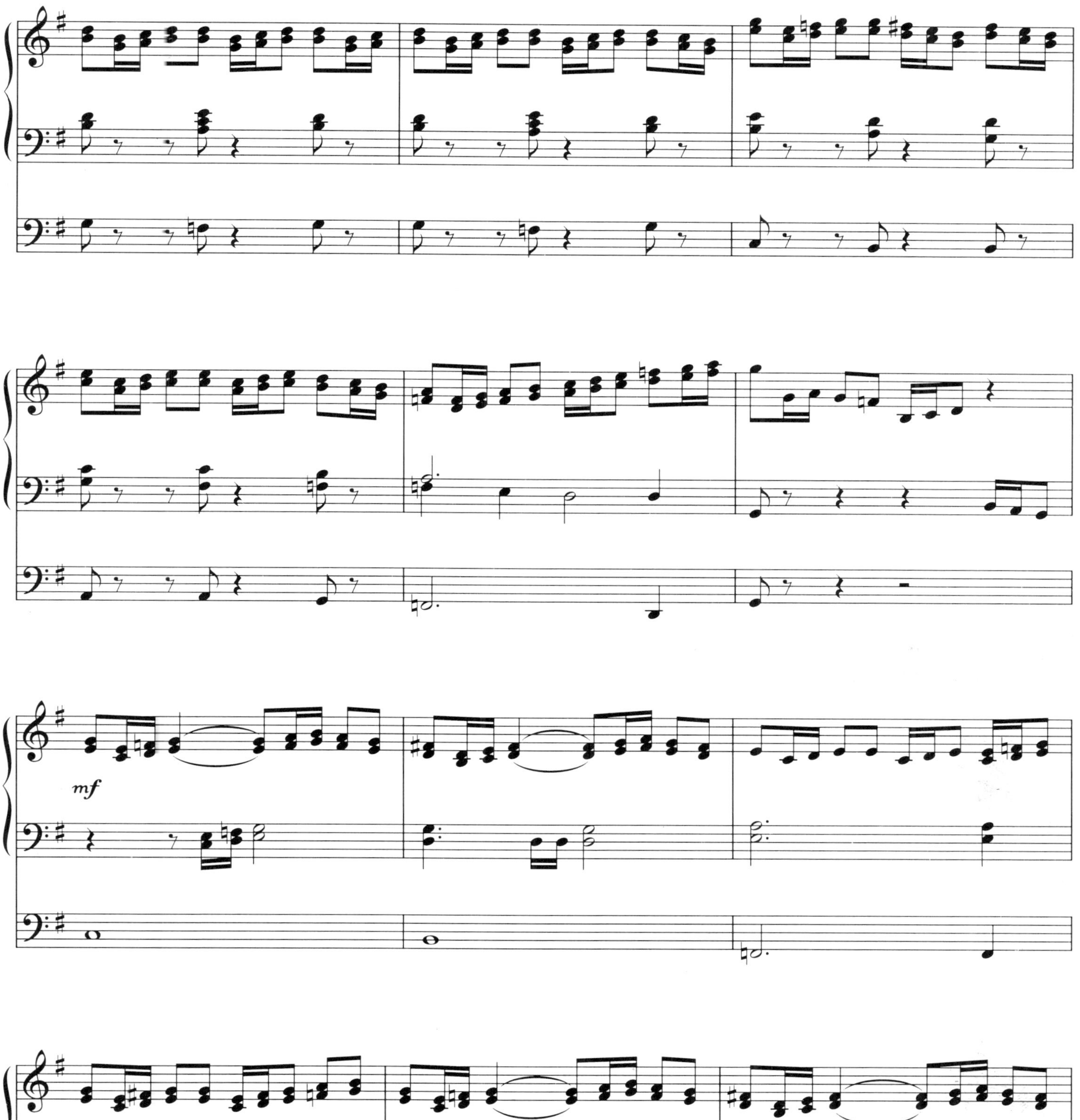
mf
mf

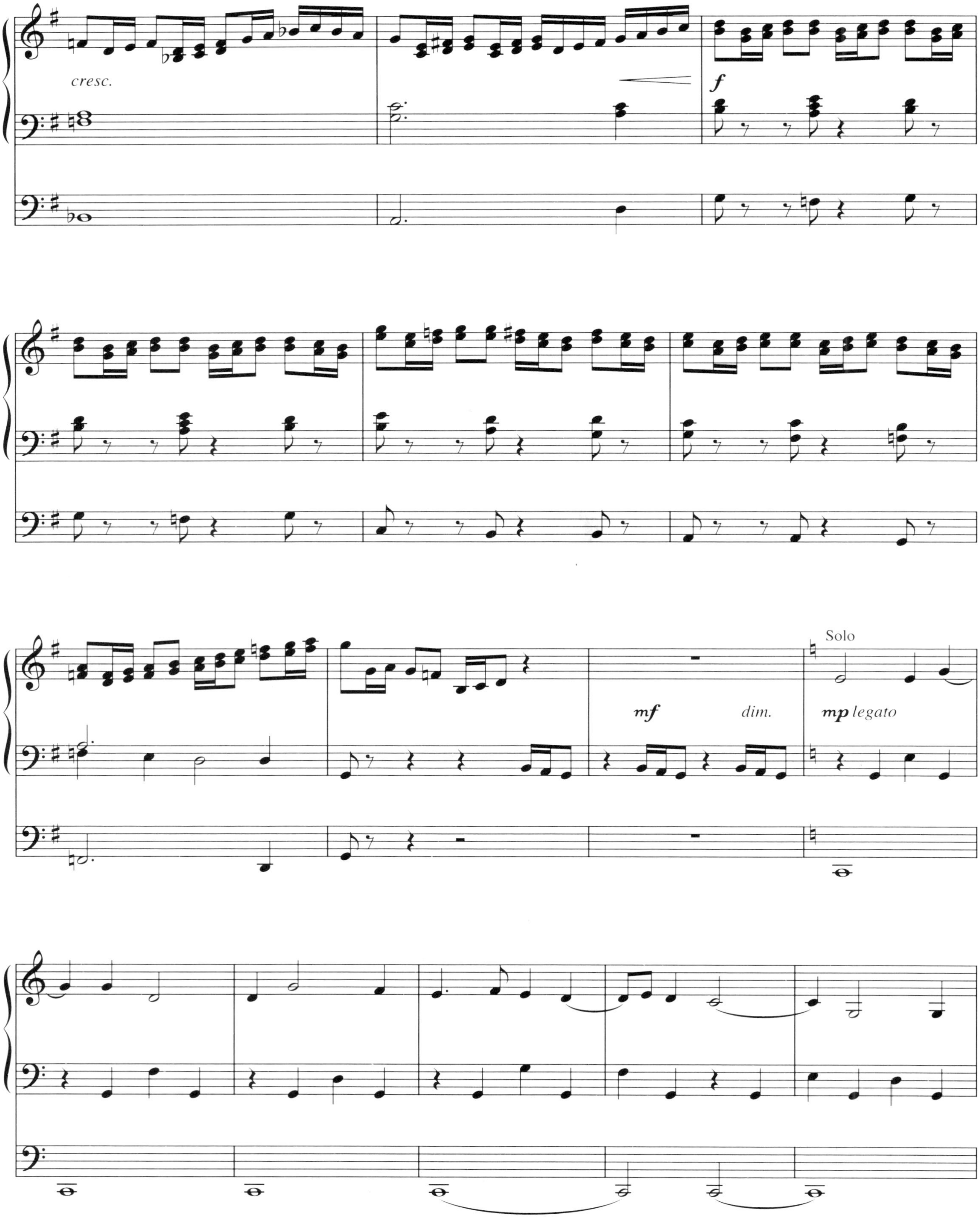

cresc.
f
mf
dim.
Solo
mp legato

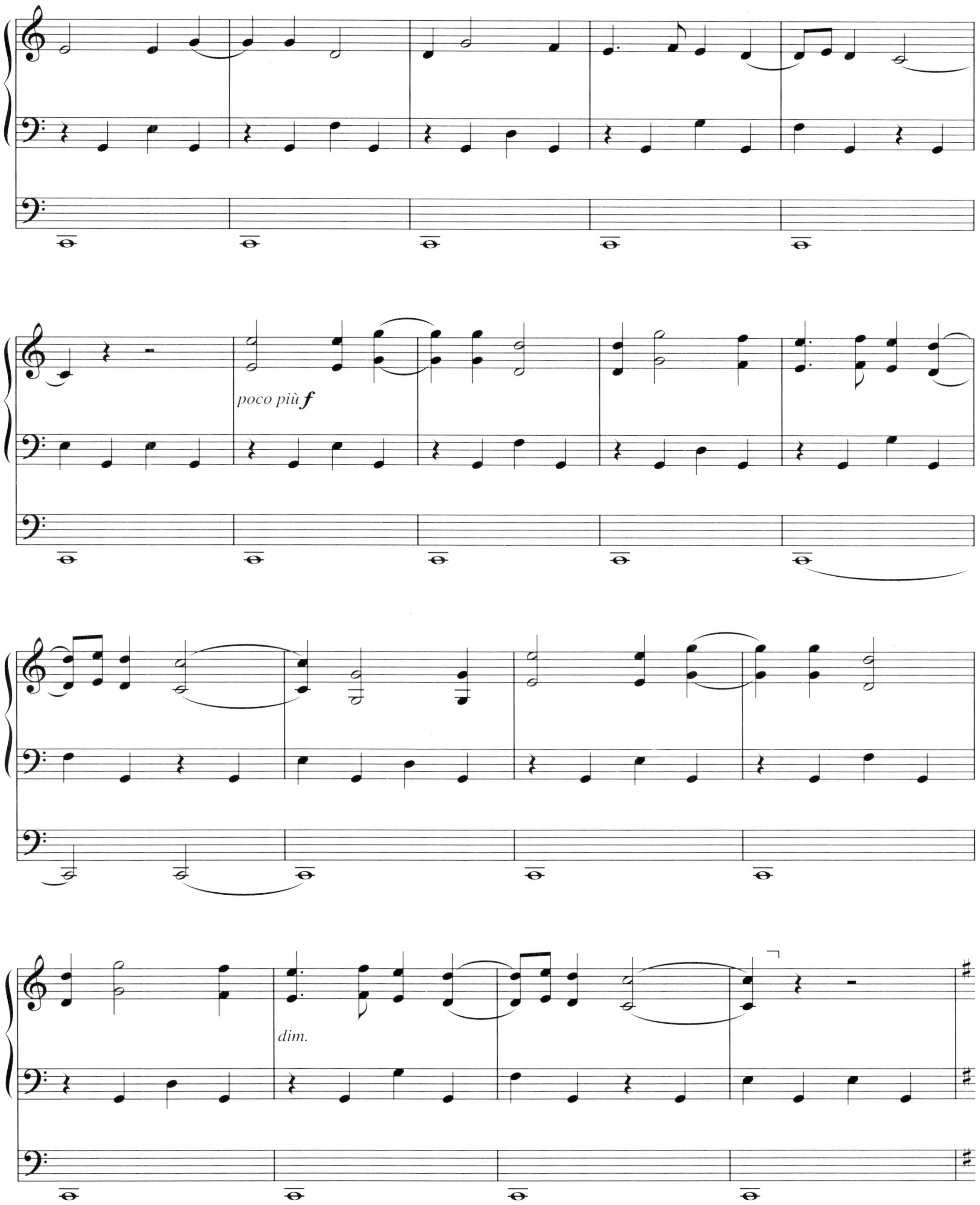
poco più f
dim.

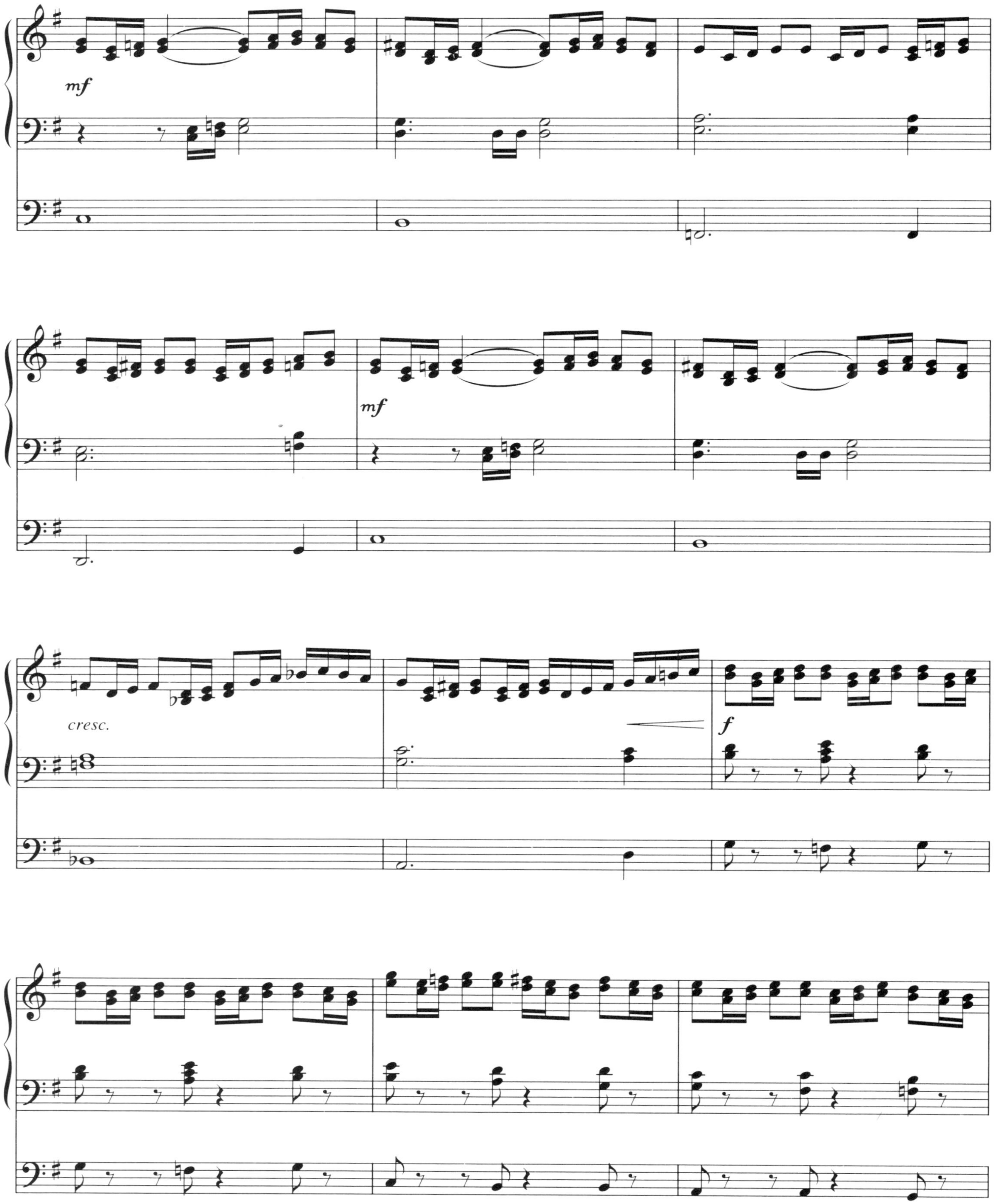
mf
mf
cresc.
f

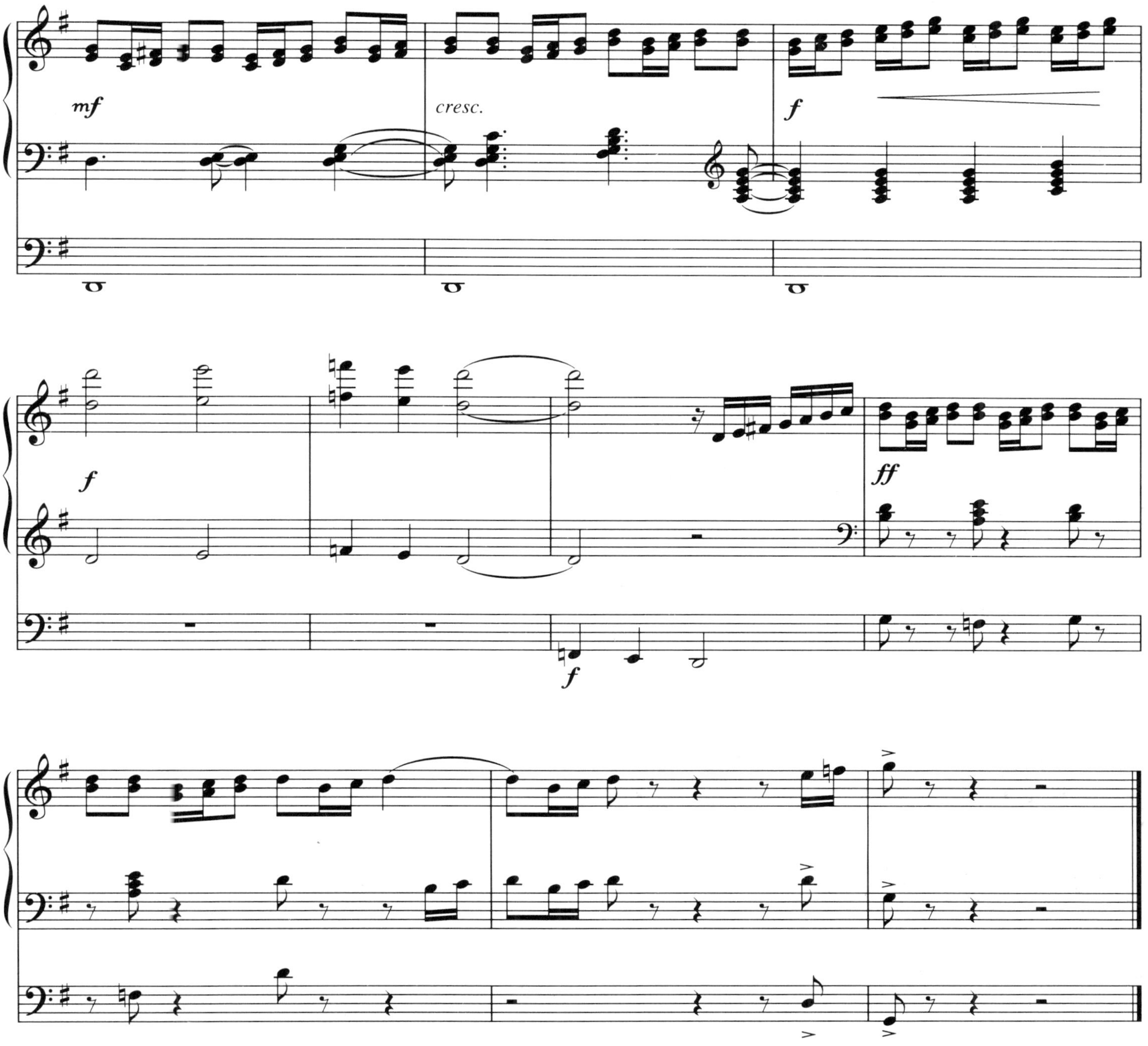
mf
cresc.
f
f
f
ff

LIGHT OF THE NATIONS

Andrew Moore

Based on the plainsong 'Lumen ad revelationem gentium'.

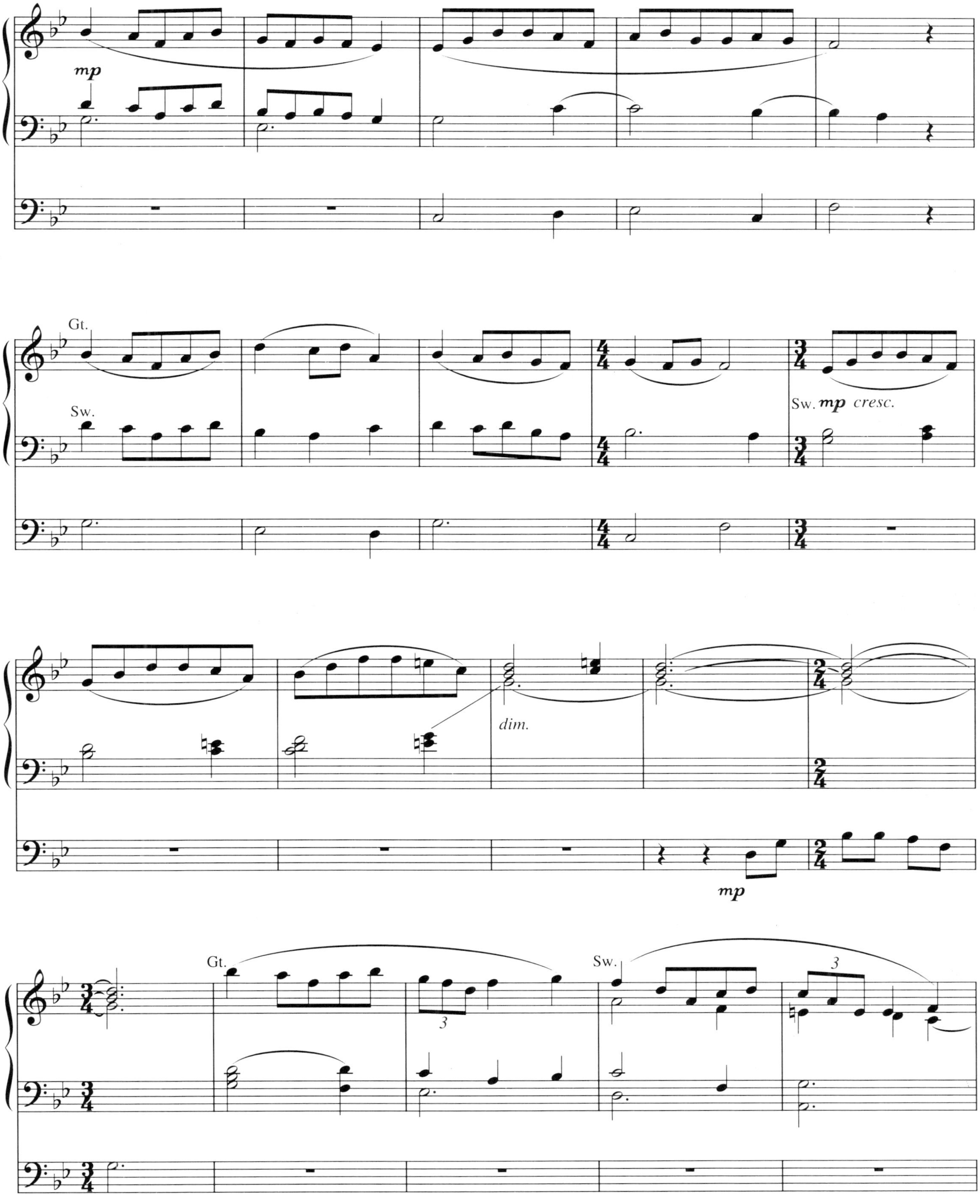
mp
Gt.
Sw.
Sw. mp cresc.
dim.
mp
Gt.
Sw.
3

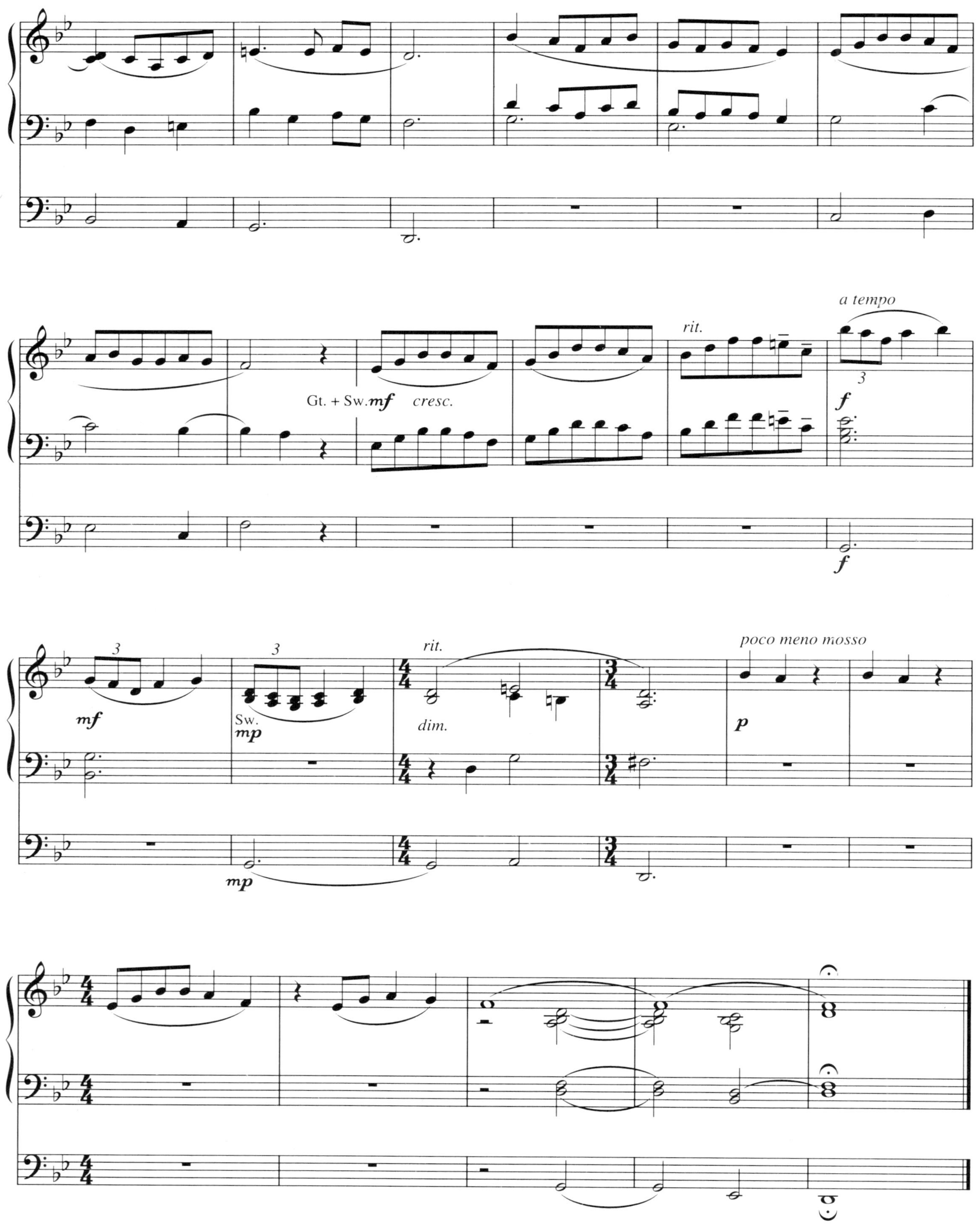
Gt. + Sw. mf
cresc.
rit.
a tempo
f
mf
Sw.
mp
dim.
poco meno mosso
p

LENTEN PASSACAGLIA

Richard Pantcheff

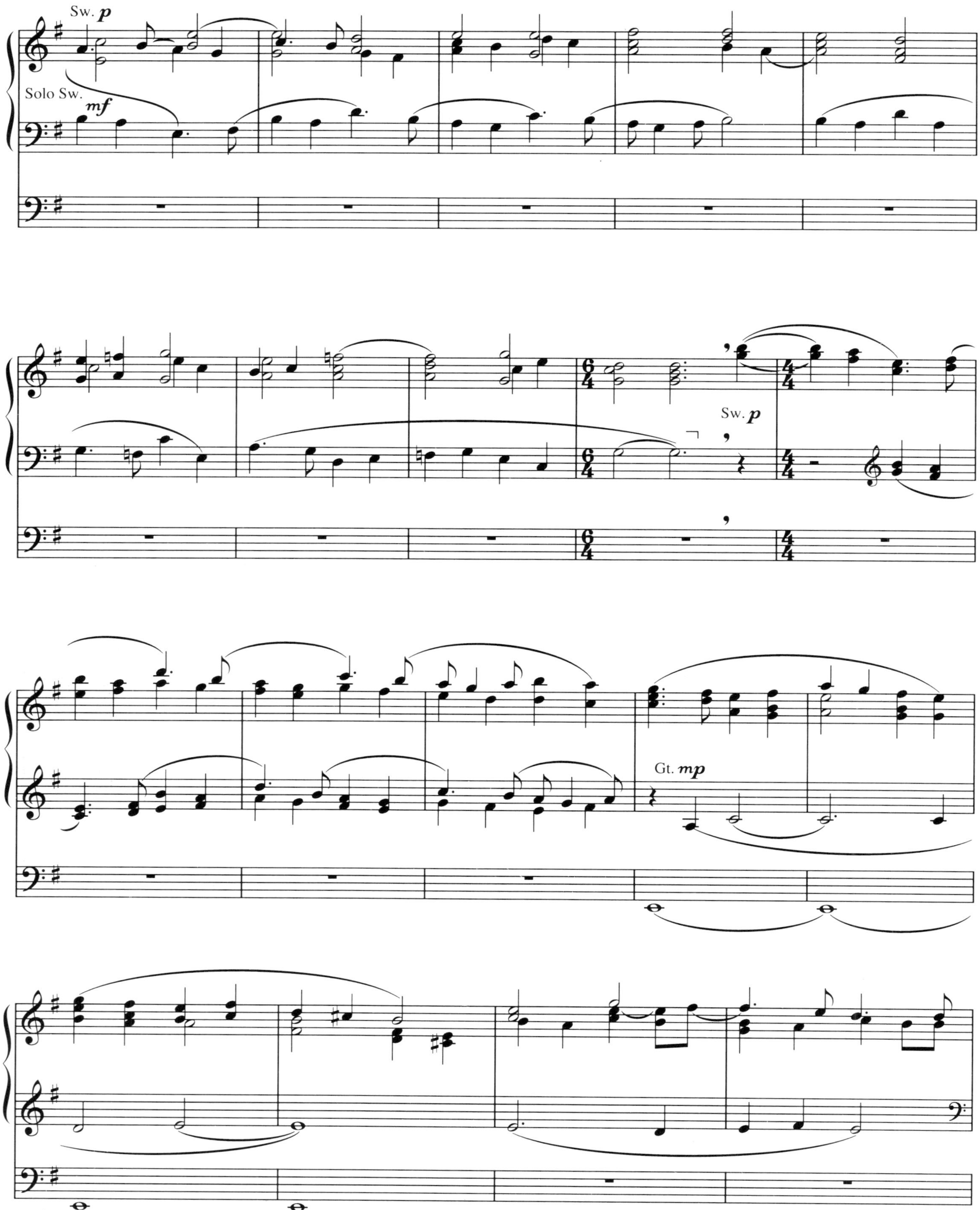
Sw. p
Solo Sw.
mf
Sw. p
Gt. mp

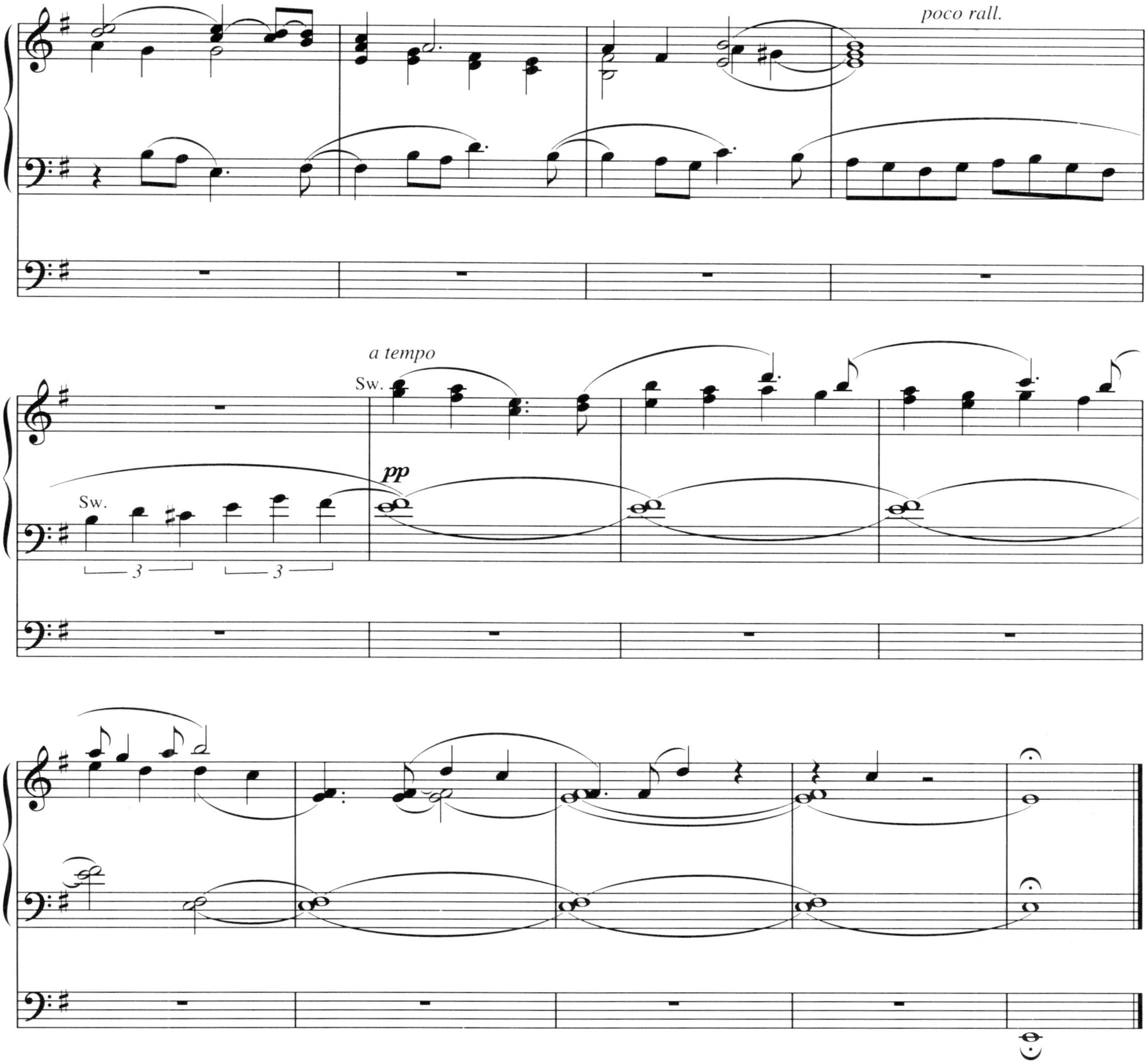
poco rall.
a tempo
Sw.
pp
Sw.
3
3

MEDITATION FOR ASH WEDNESDAY

June Nixon

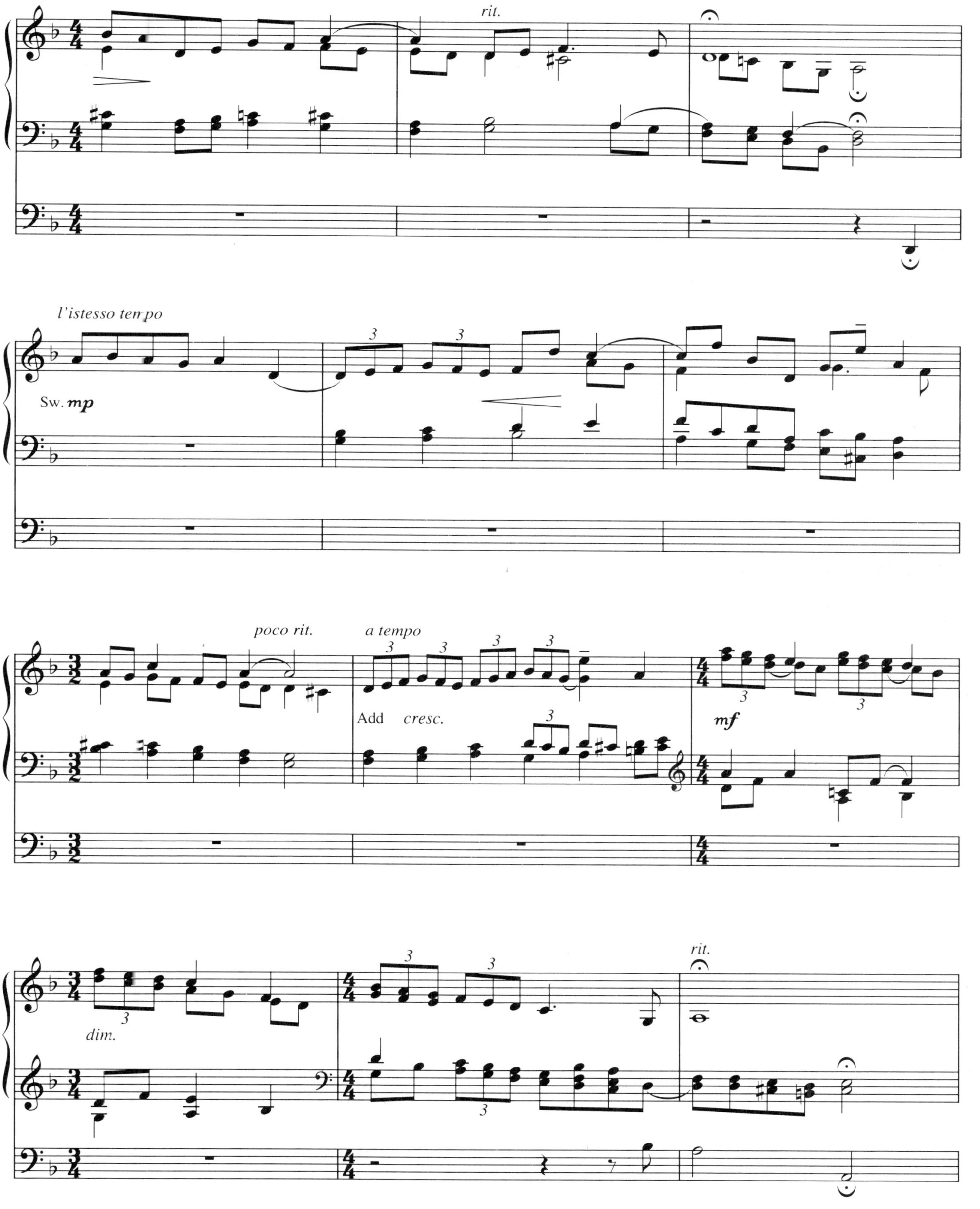
rit.
l'istesso tempo
Sw. mp
poco rit.
a tempo
Add
cresc.
mf
dim.
rit.

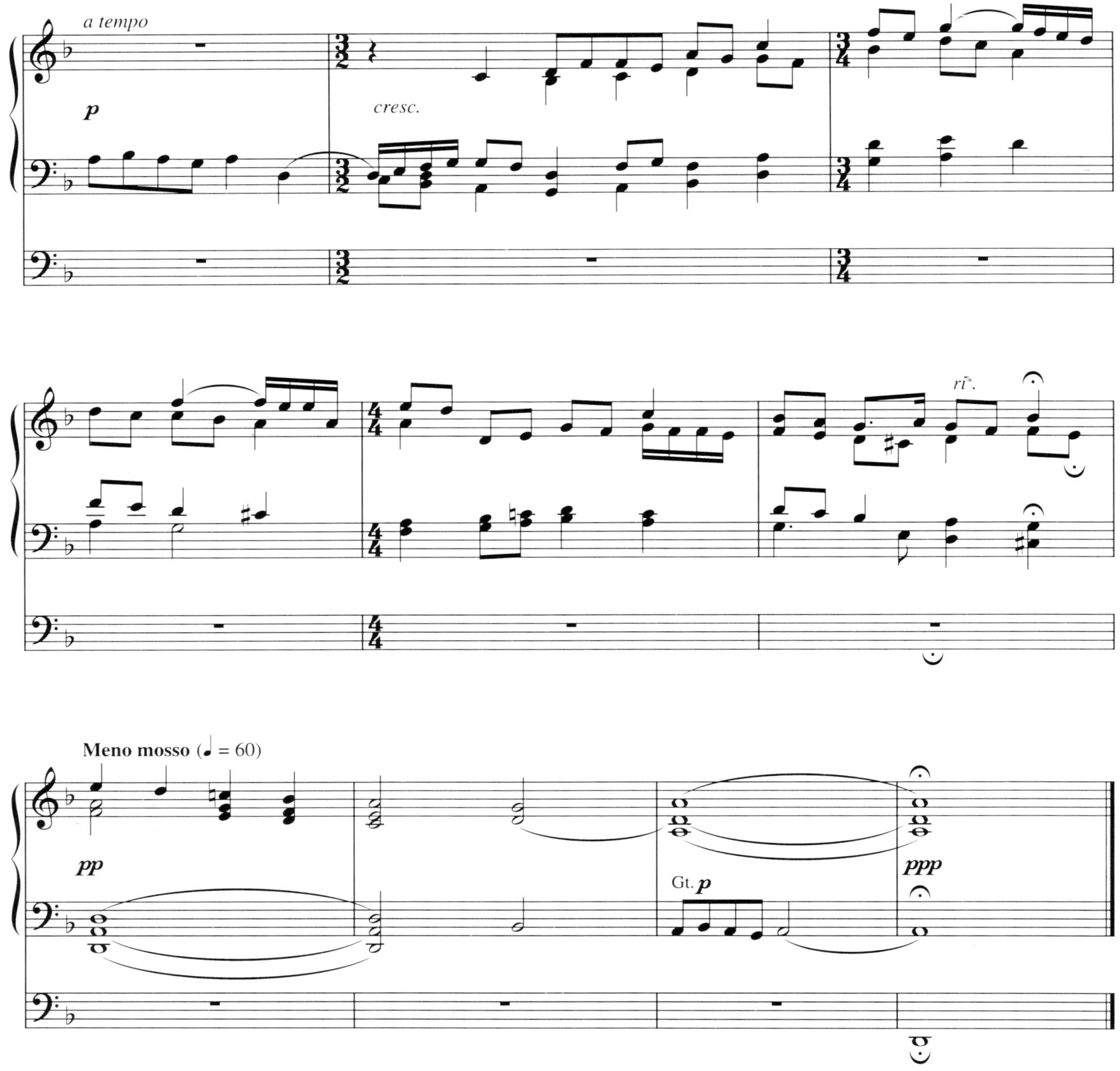
a tempo
p
cresc.
rit.
Meno mosso (♩ = 60)
pp
Gt. p
ppp

REFLECTIVE PRELUDE

James Patten

Sw. Stopped Diapason 8', Strings 8'
Gt. Stopped Flutes 8'
Ped. Bourdon

Moto moderato (♩ = c. 60)

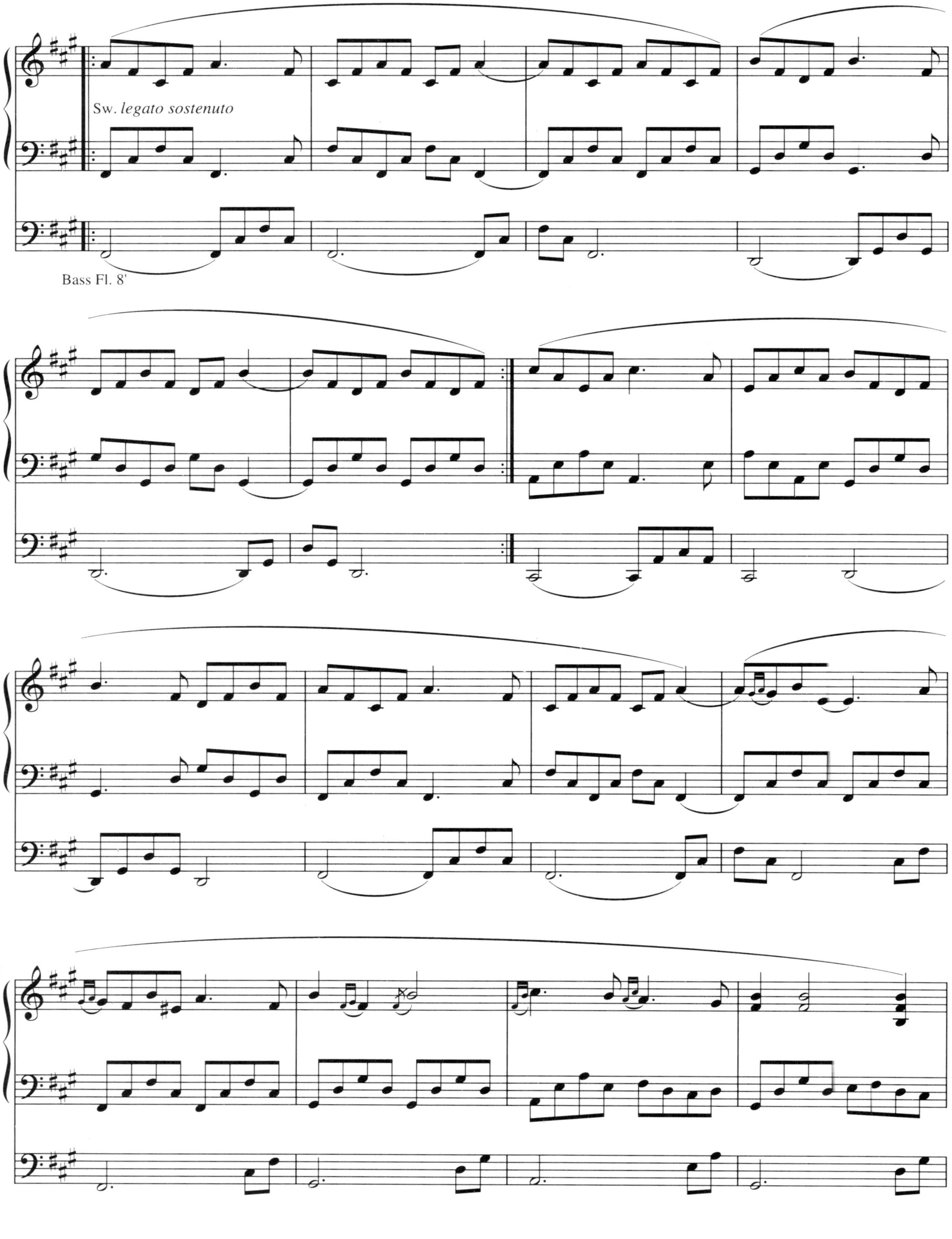

Sw. legato sostenuto
Bass Fl. 8'

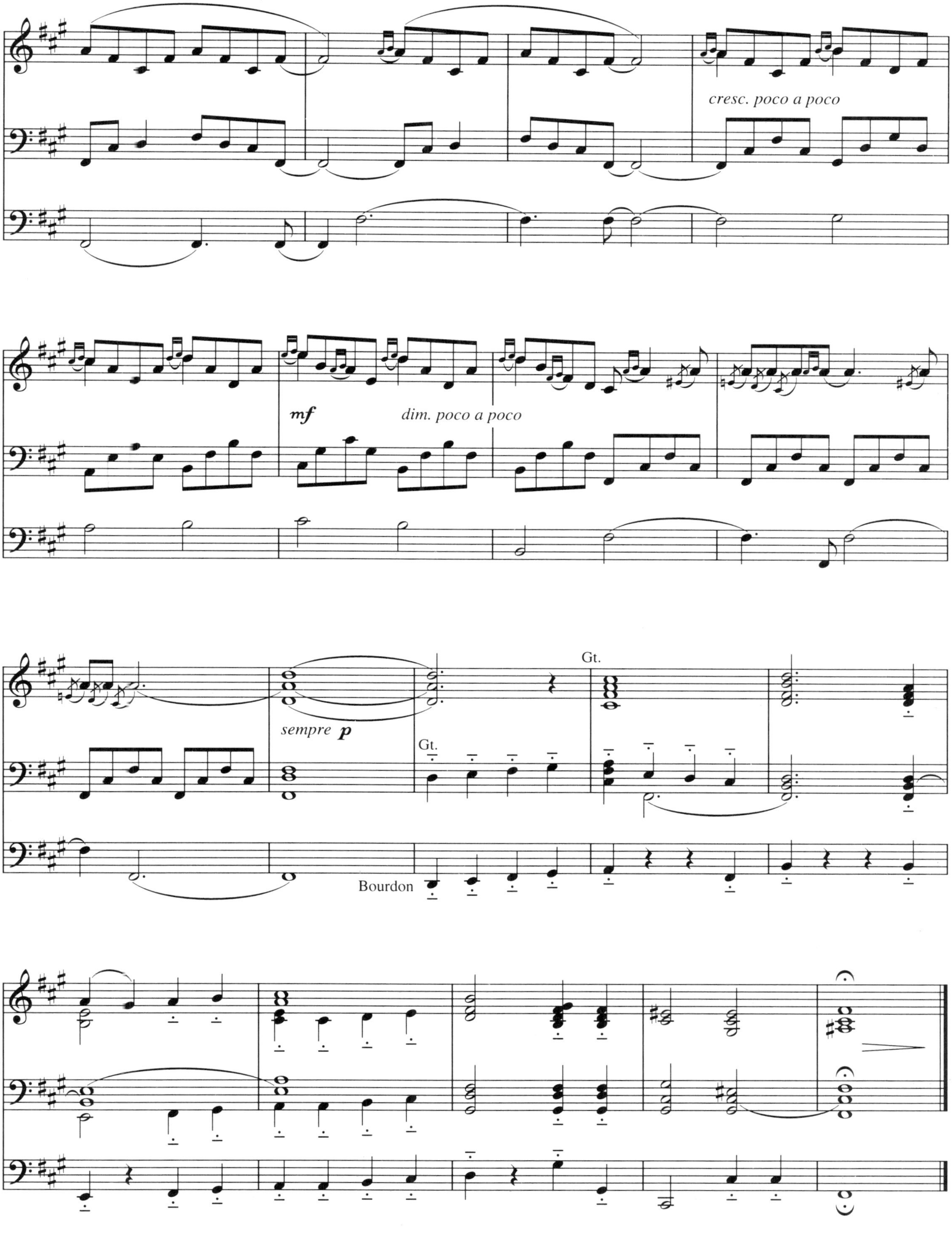

cresc. poco a poco
mf
dim. poco a poco
sempre p
Gt.
Gt.
Bourdon

SOLEMN PROCESSIONAL MARCH

Martin Setchell

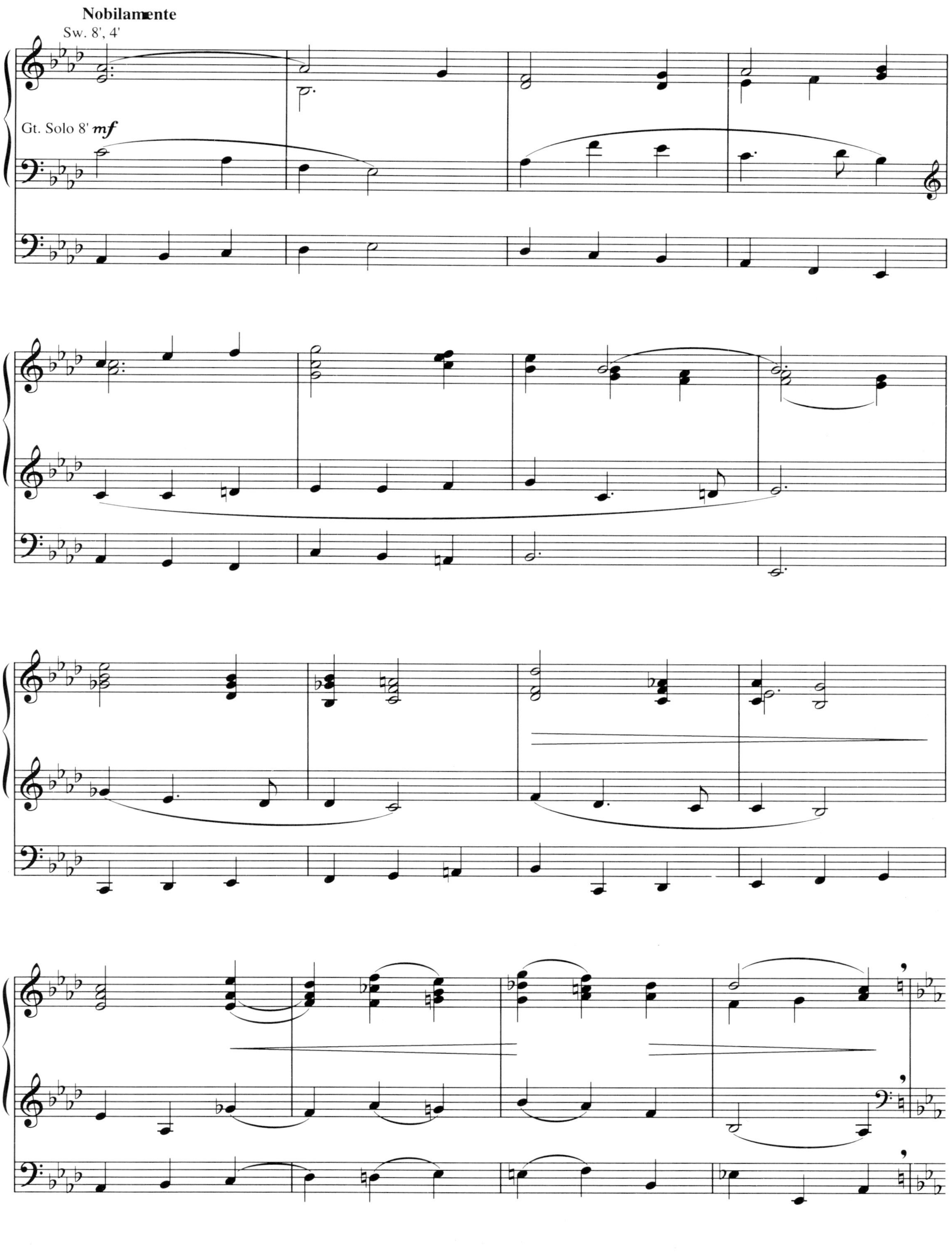
Nobilamente
Sw. 8', 4'
Gt. Solo 8' mf

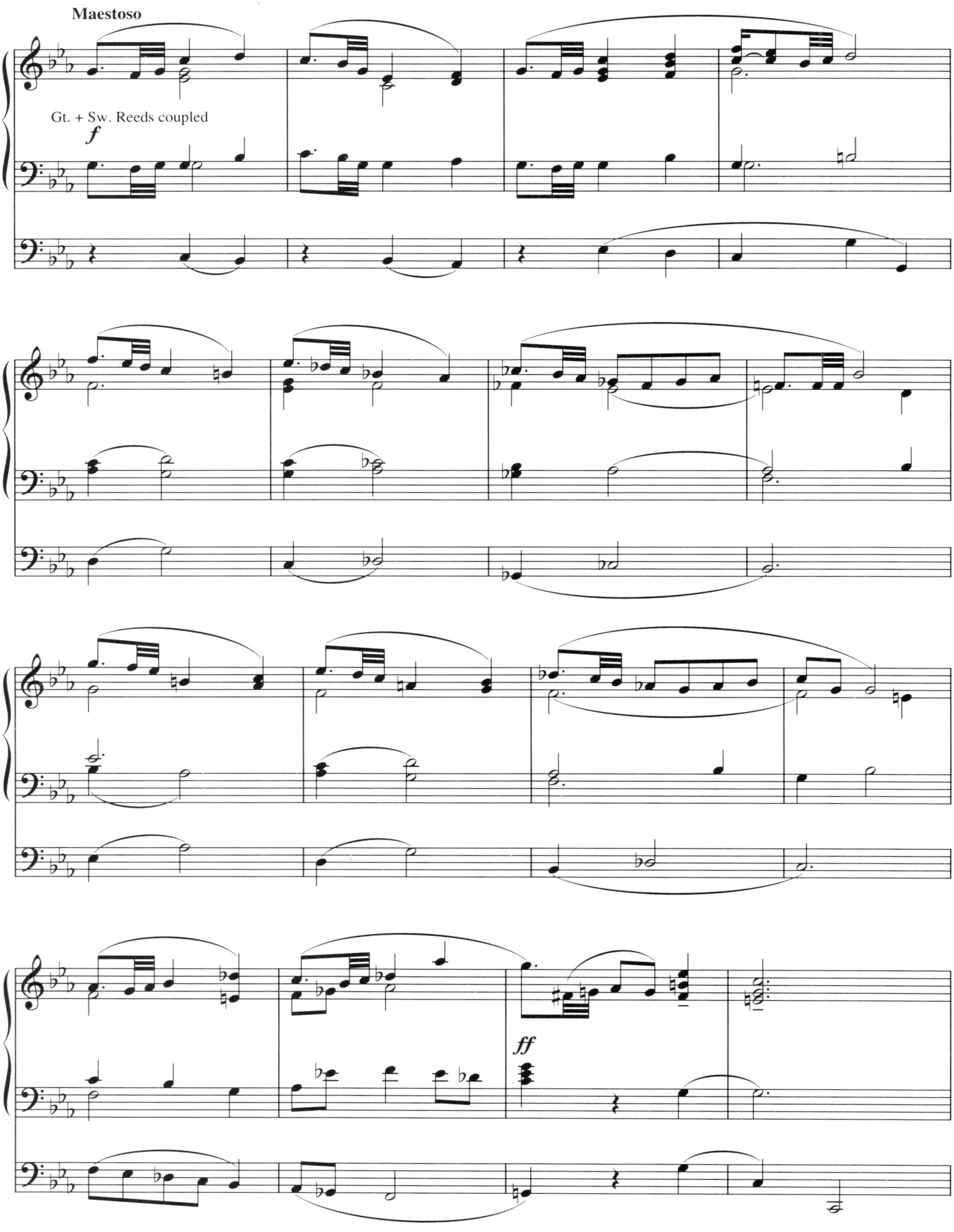
Maestoso
Gt. + Sw. Reeds coupled
f
ff

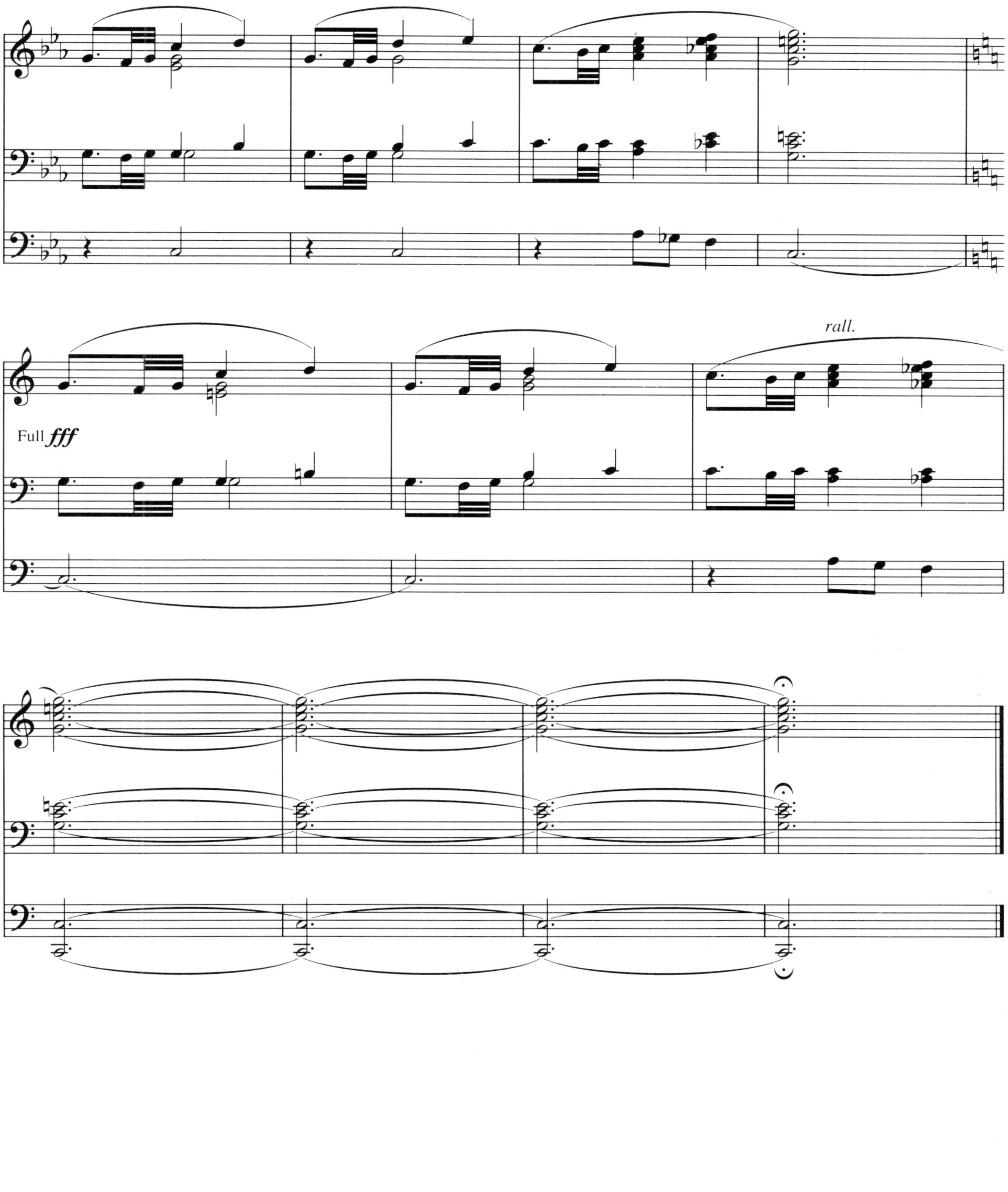
Full fff
rall.

Dedicated to Kevin Mayhew

NUMERALIS

Richard Proulx

Sw. Strings 8'
Gt. Flute 8'
Ped. Flute 4'

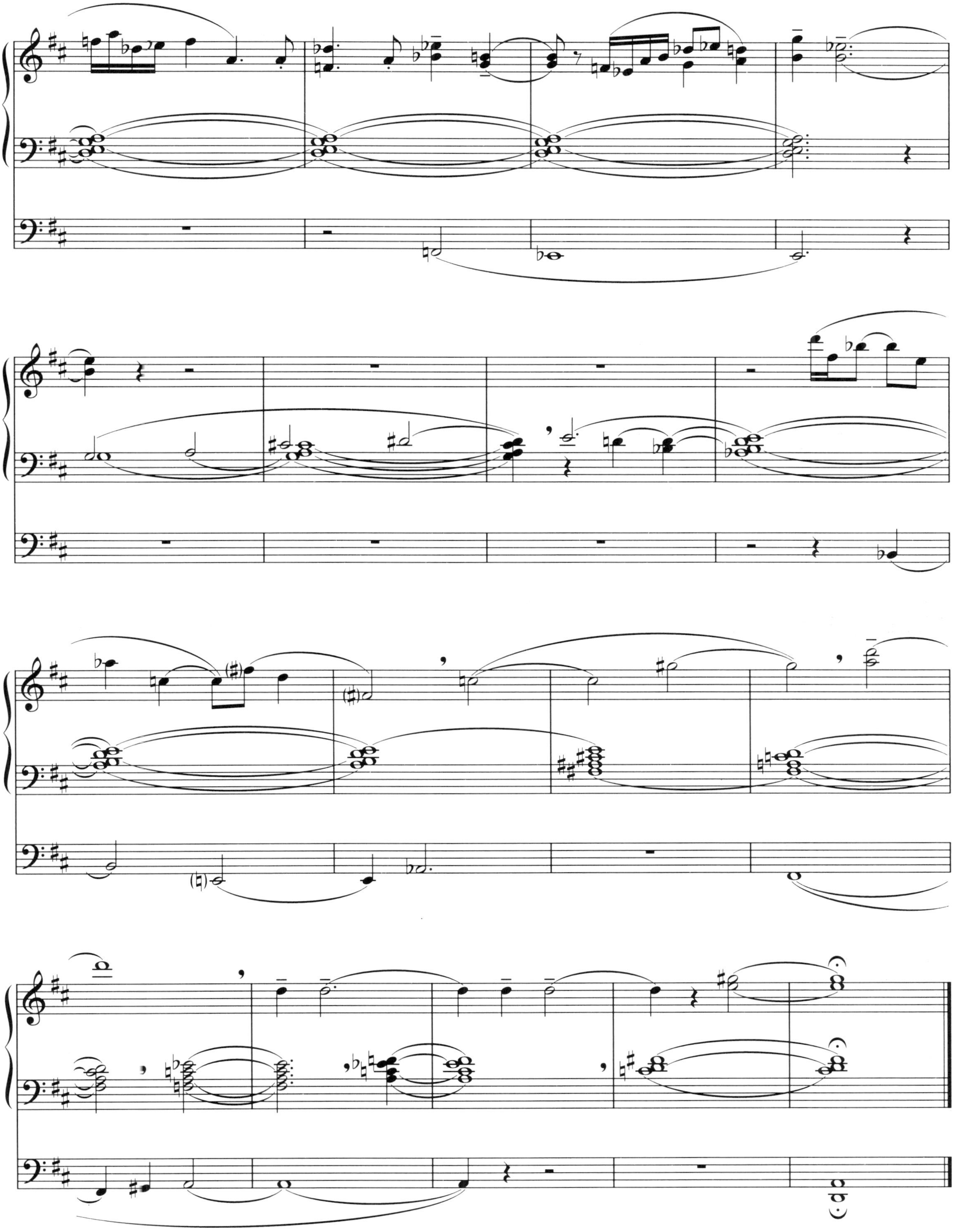

EDEN

Betty Roe

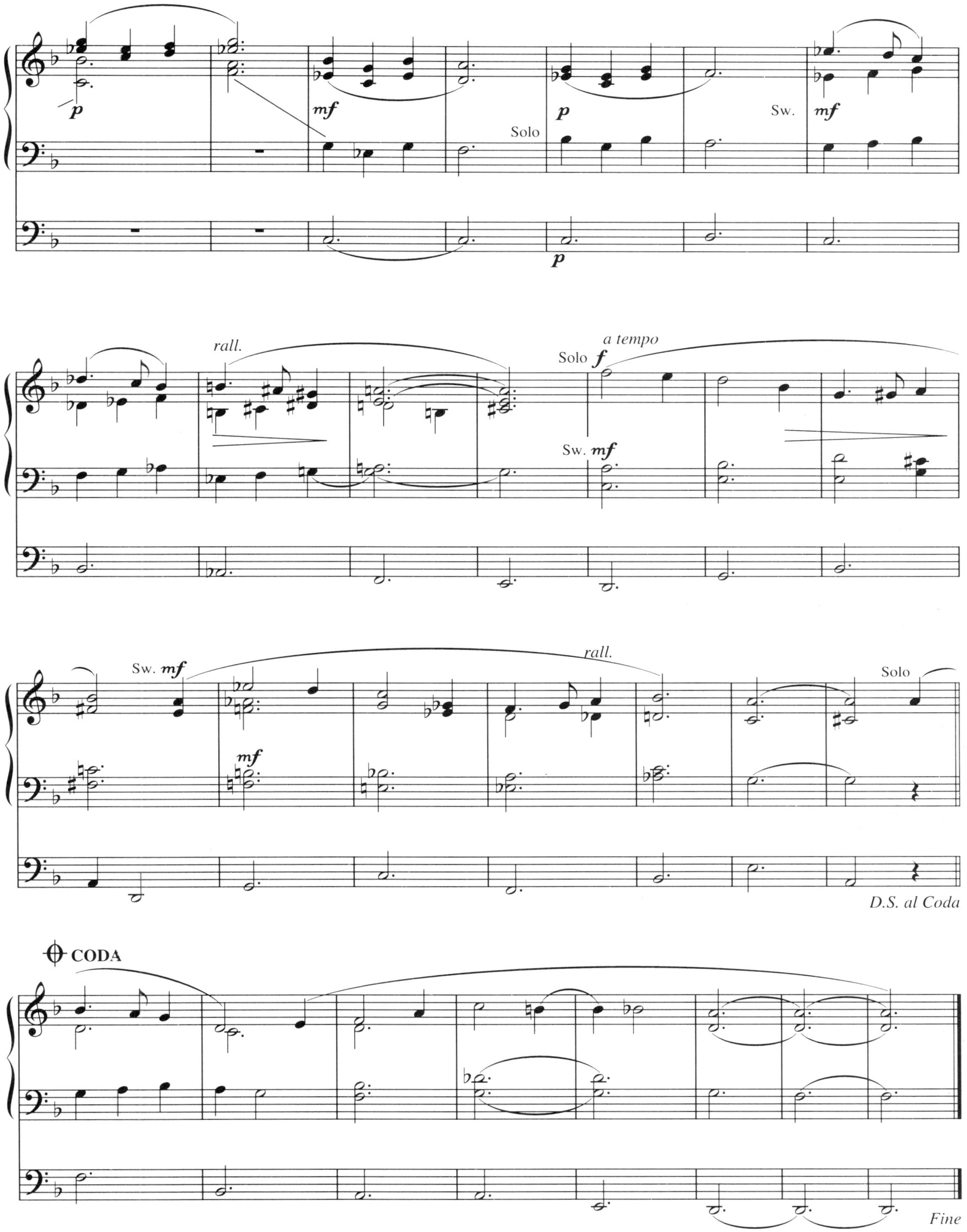
Solo
Sw.
rall.
a tempo
Solo
Sw.
Sw.
rall.
Solo
D.S. al Coda
CODA
Fine

UBI CARITAS

Colin Mawby

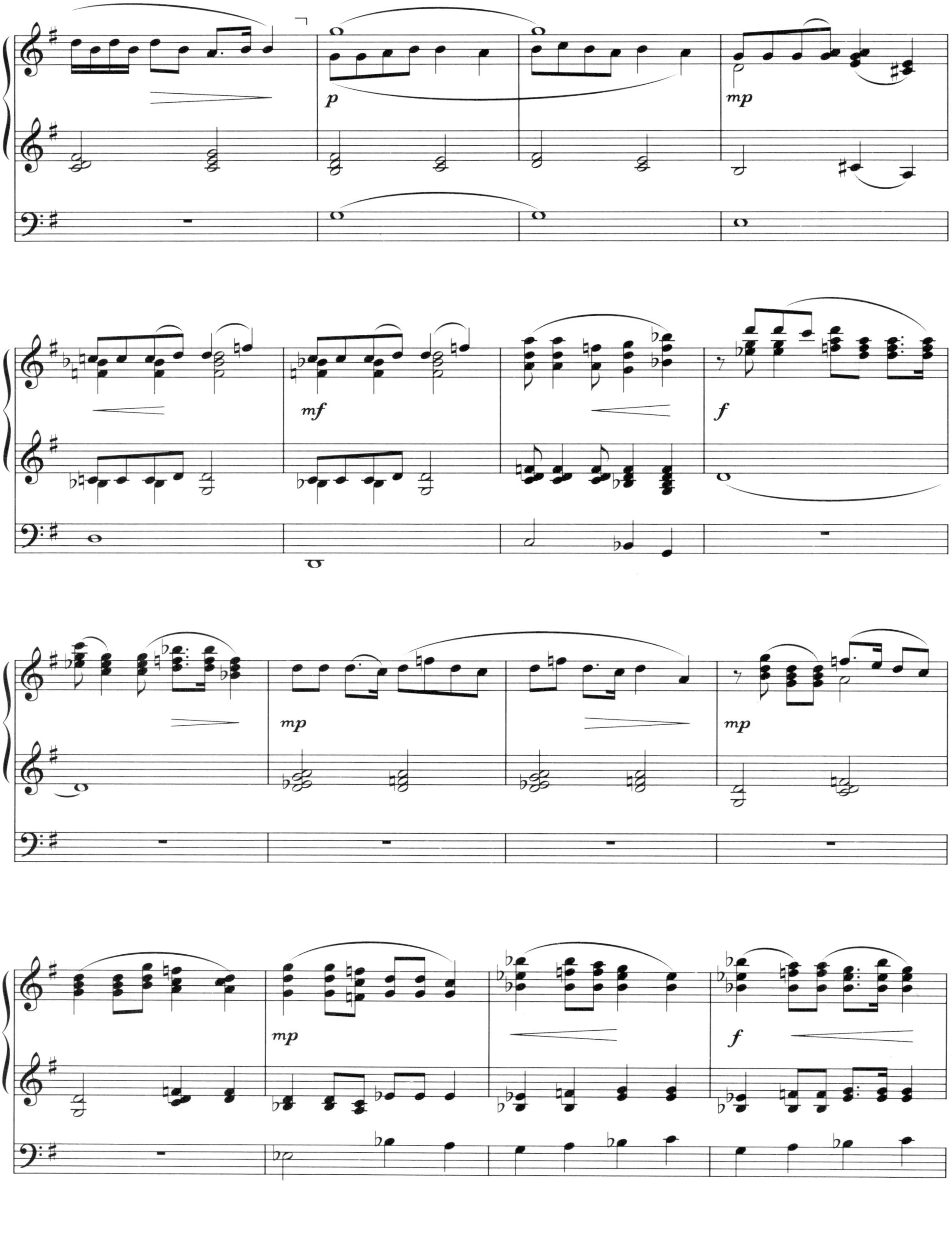
p
mp
mf
f
mp
mp
mp
f

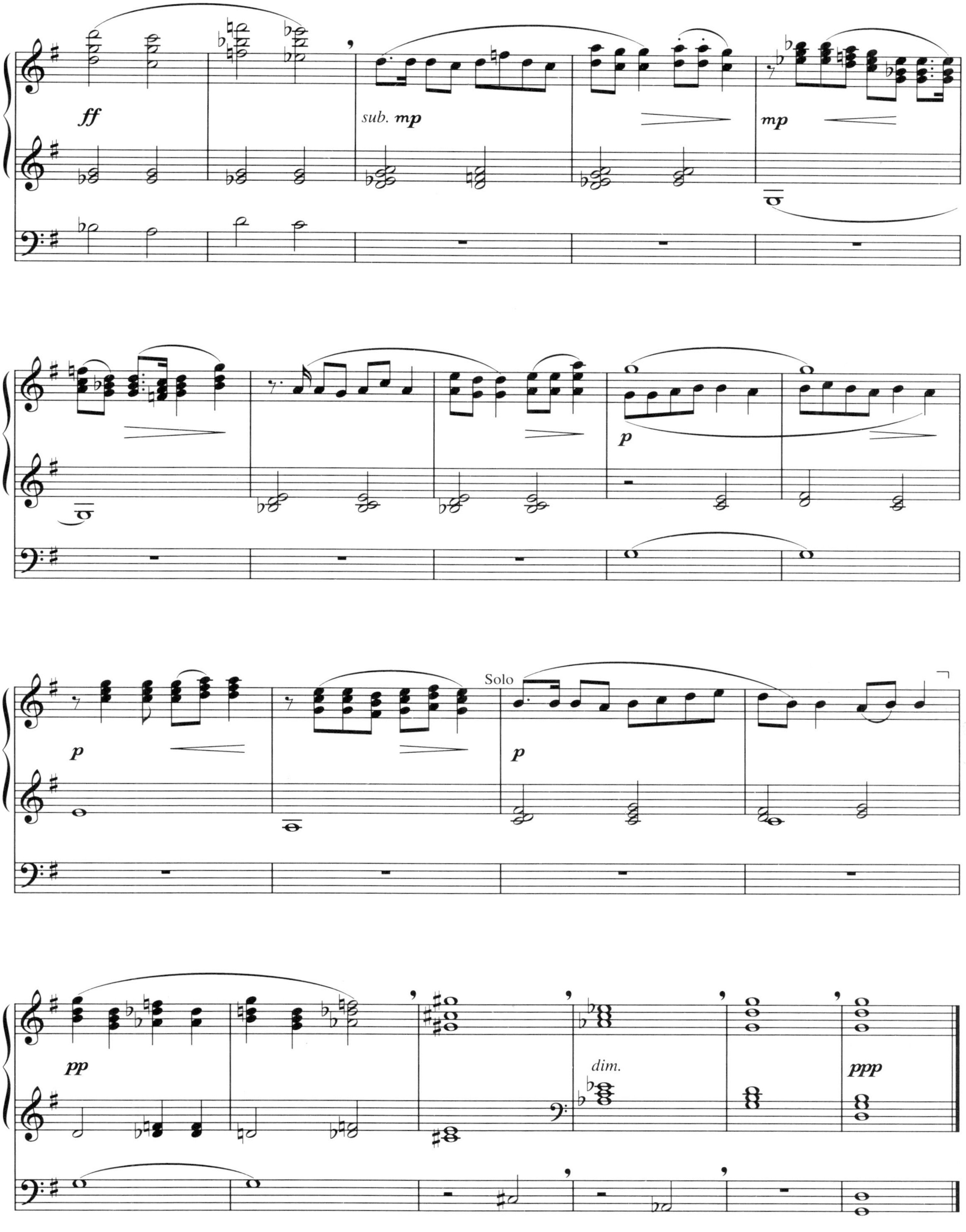
ff
sub. mp
mp
p
p
Solo
p
pp
dim.
ppp

PALM SUNDAY PROCESSIONAL

Christopher Tambling

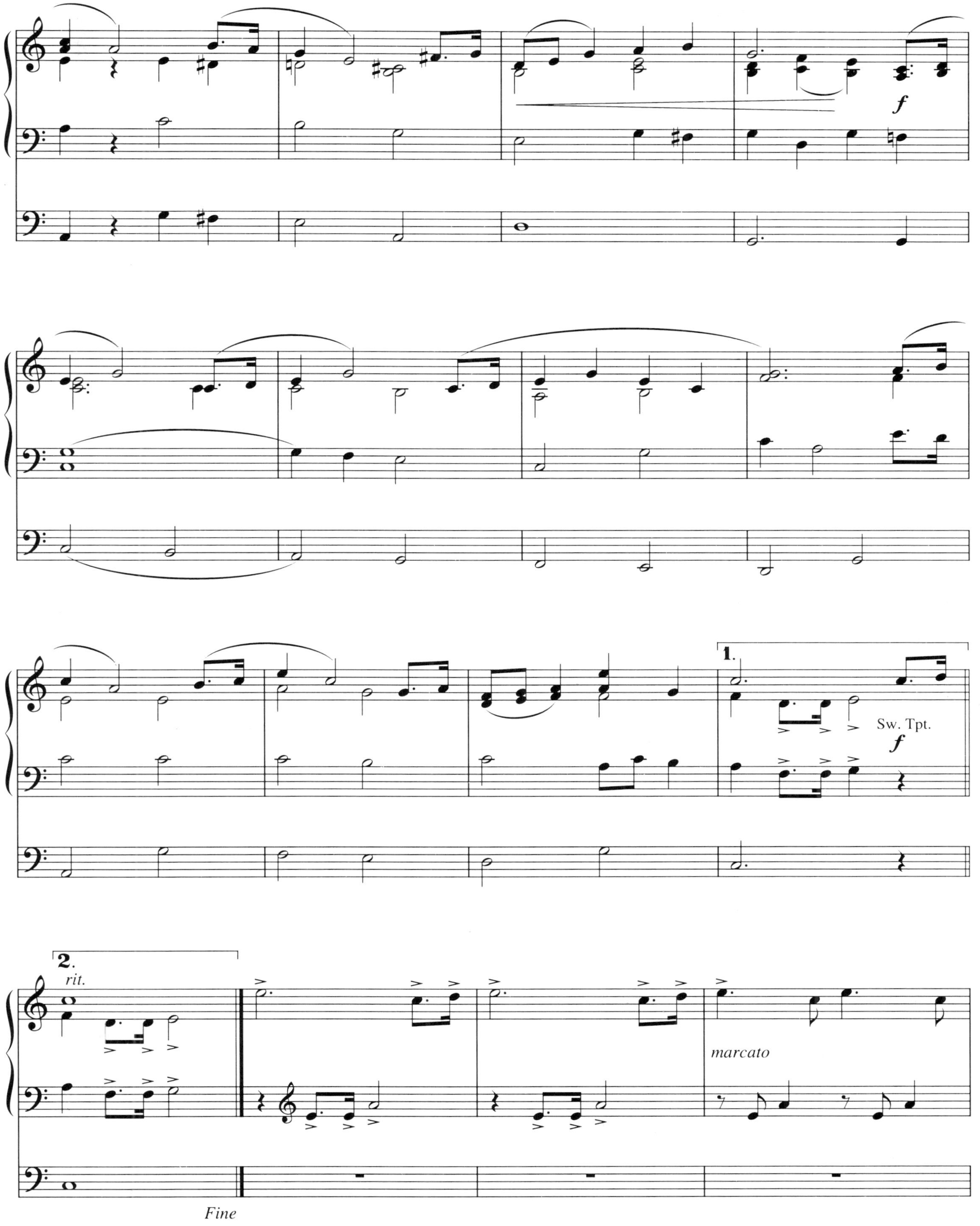
f
1.
Sw. Tpt.
f
2.
rit.
marcato
Fine

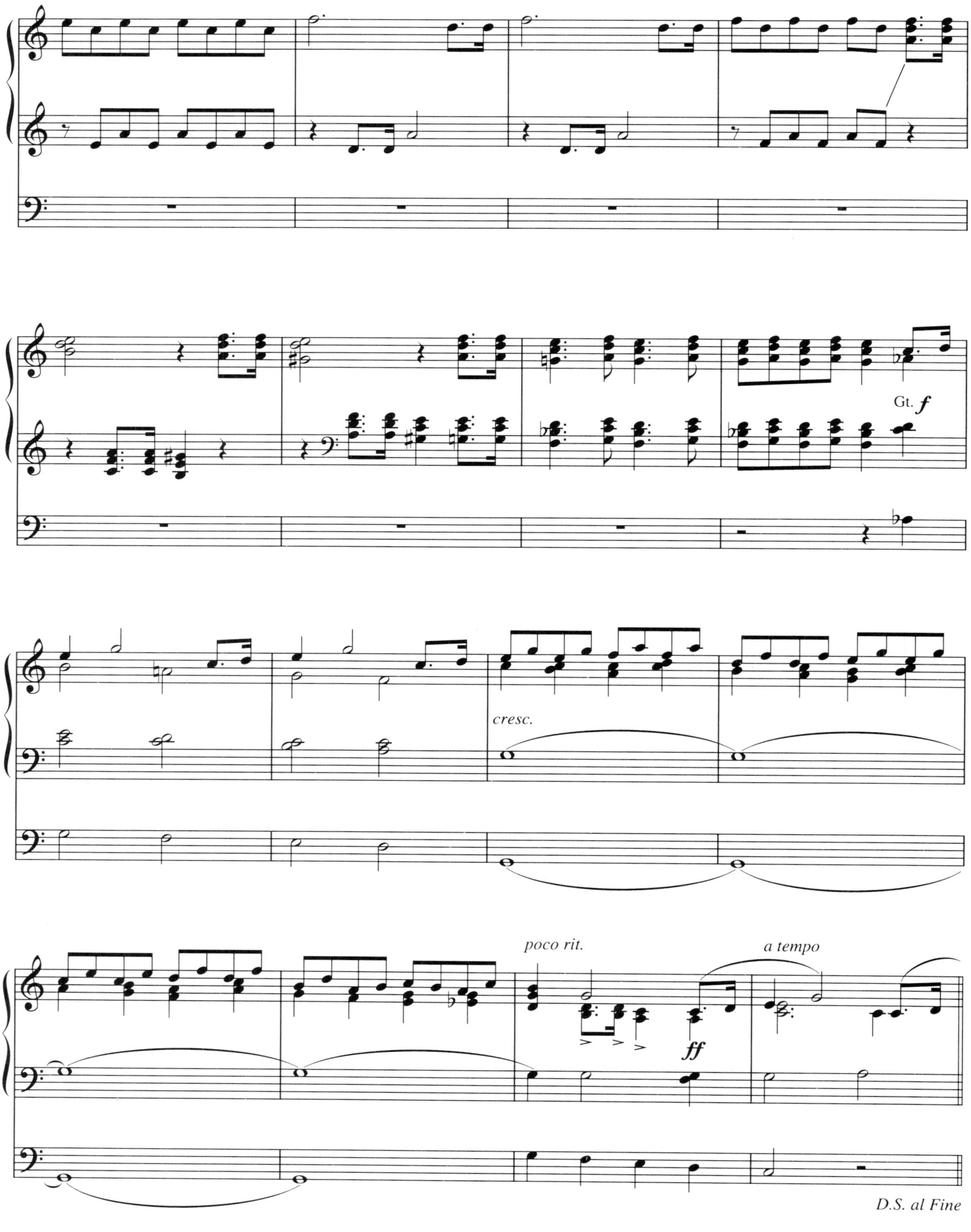
Gt. f
cresc.
poco rit.
a tempo
ff
D.S. al Fine

'IT IS FINISHED'

Stanley Vann

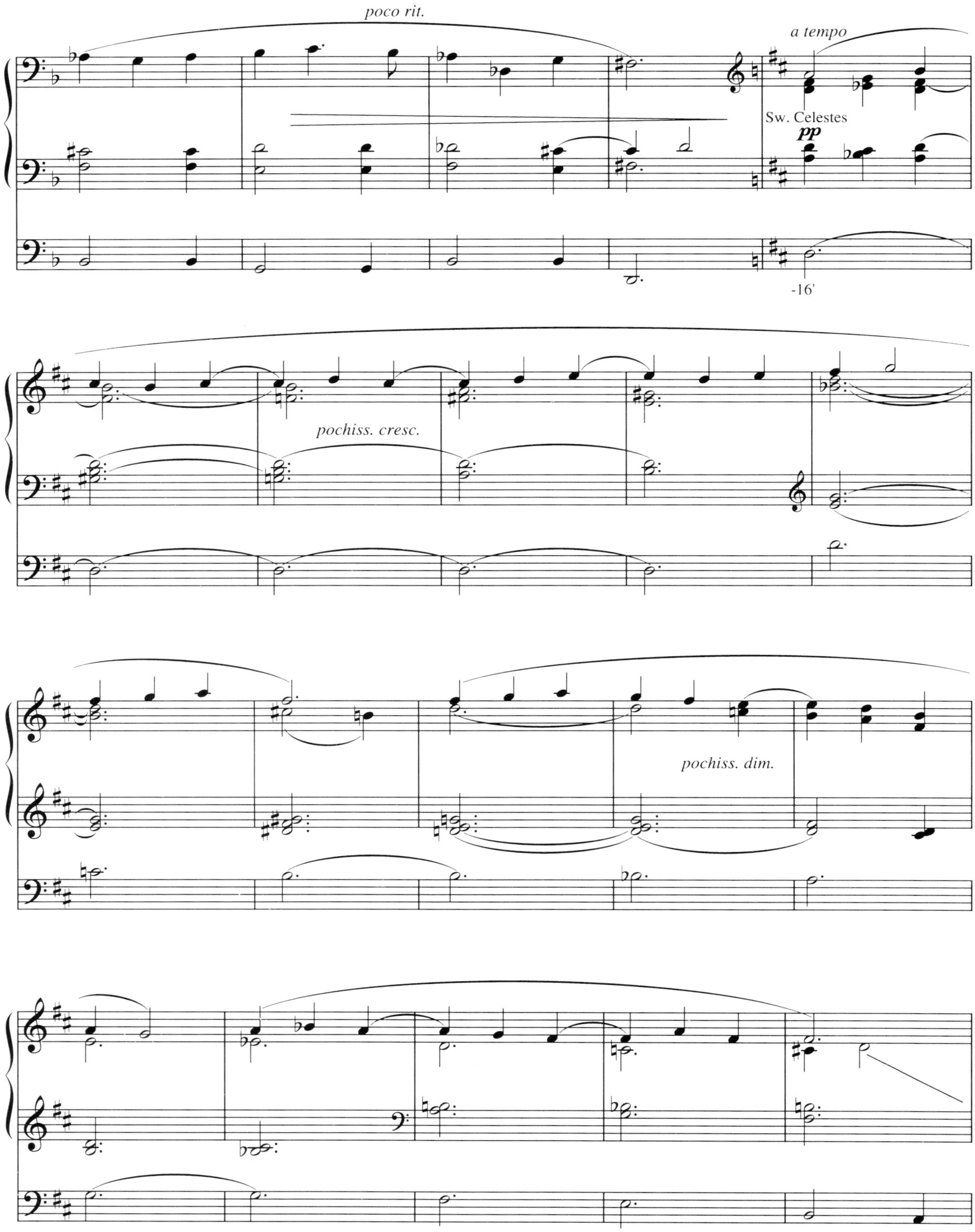
poco rit.
a tempo
Sw. Celestes
pp
-16'
pochiss. cresc.
pochiss. dim.

poco rit.
Solo
mp
a tempo
ten.
dim.
+16'
p echo
mf
molto rit.
molto dim.
pp

RESURRECTION DANCE

Adrian Vernon Fish

Allegro vivo (♩ = 120)

Full *ff sempre staccato*

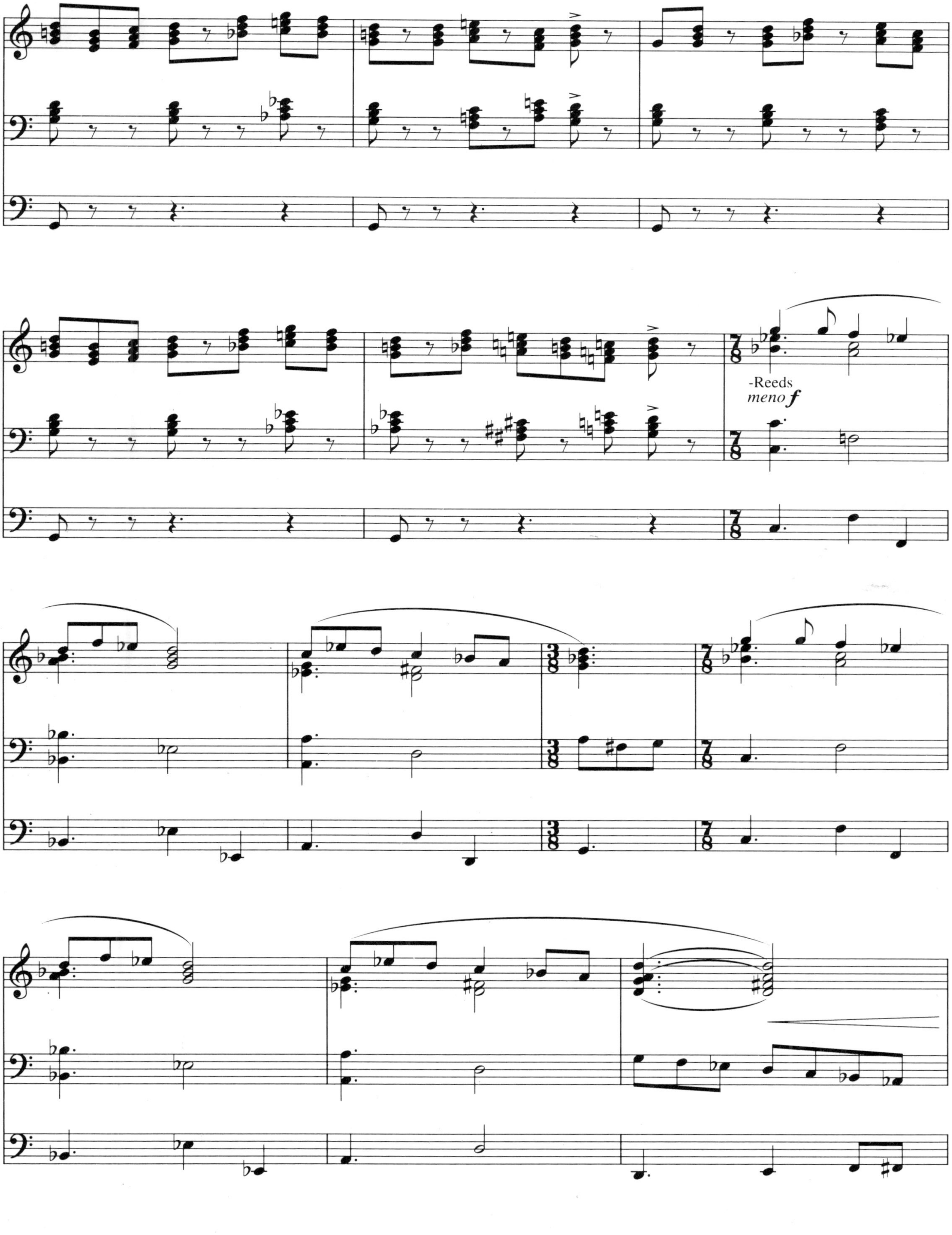
-Reeds
meno f

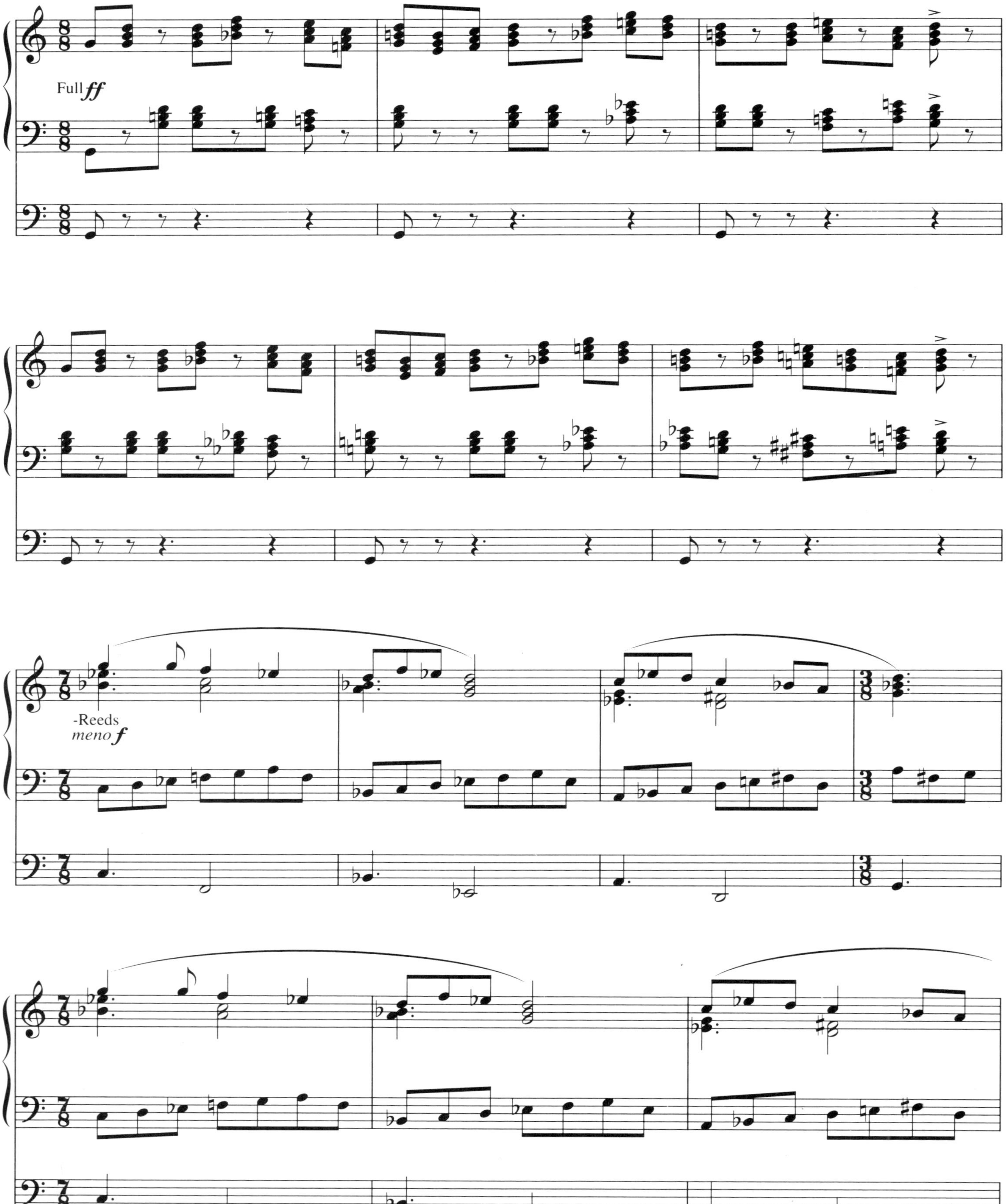
Full ff
-Reeds
meno f

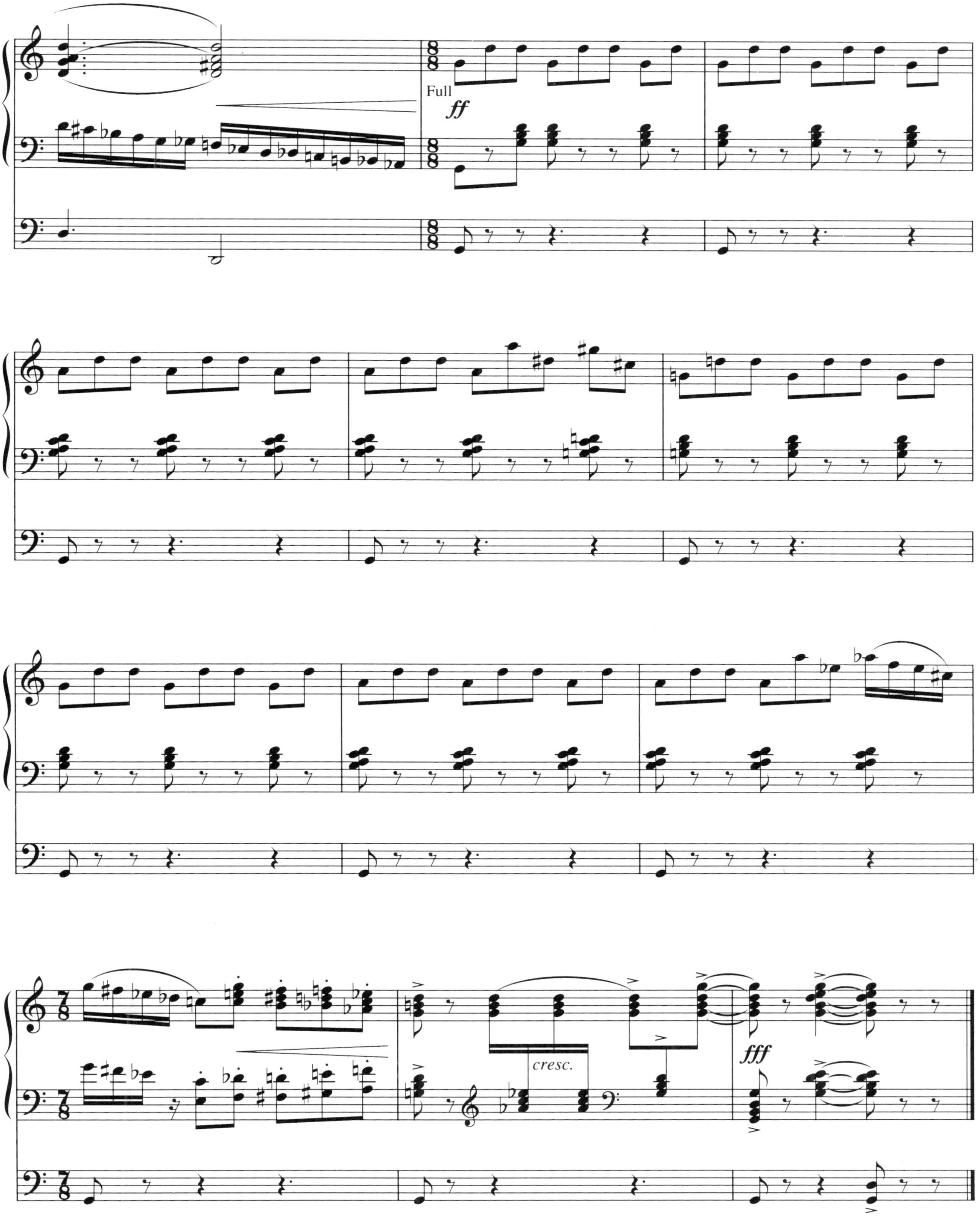
Full
ff
cresc.
fff

DUM TRANSISET SABBATUM

Andrew Gant

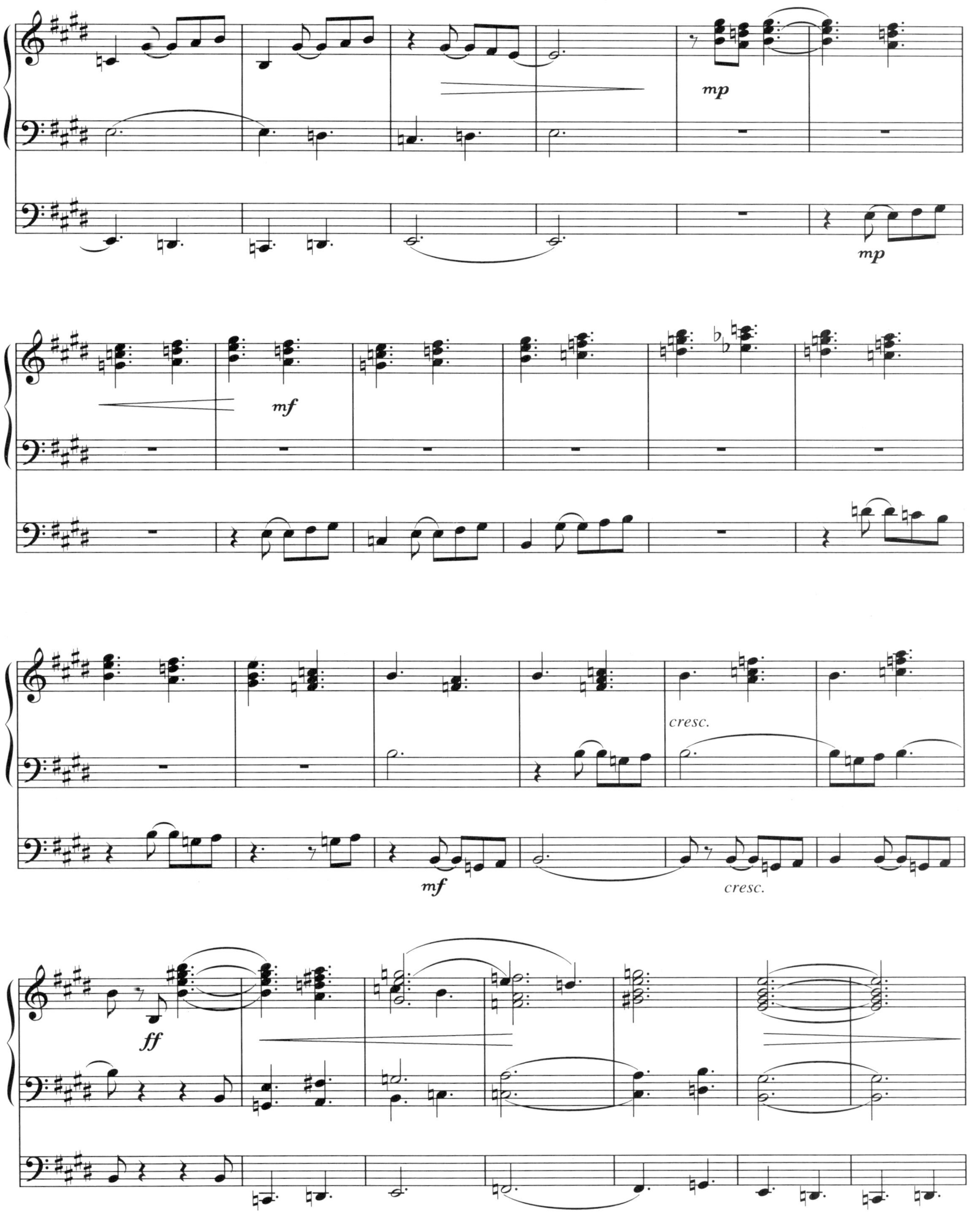
mp
mp
mf
cresc.
mf
cresc.
ff

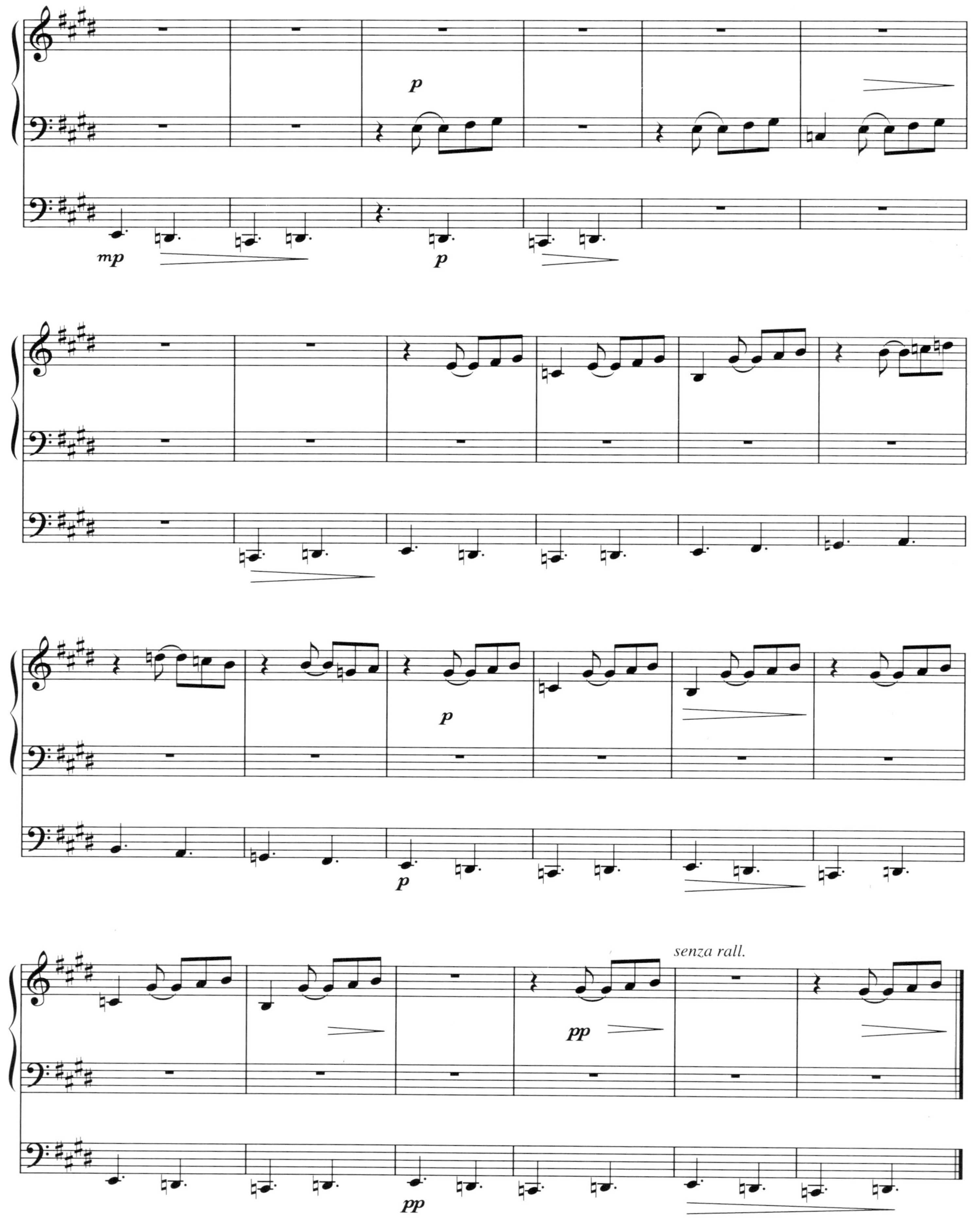
mp
p
p
p
p
p
pp
senza rall.
pp

FESTIVE JOY

Simon Clark

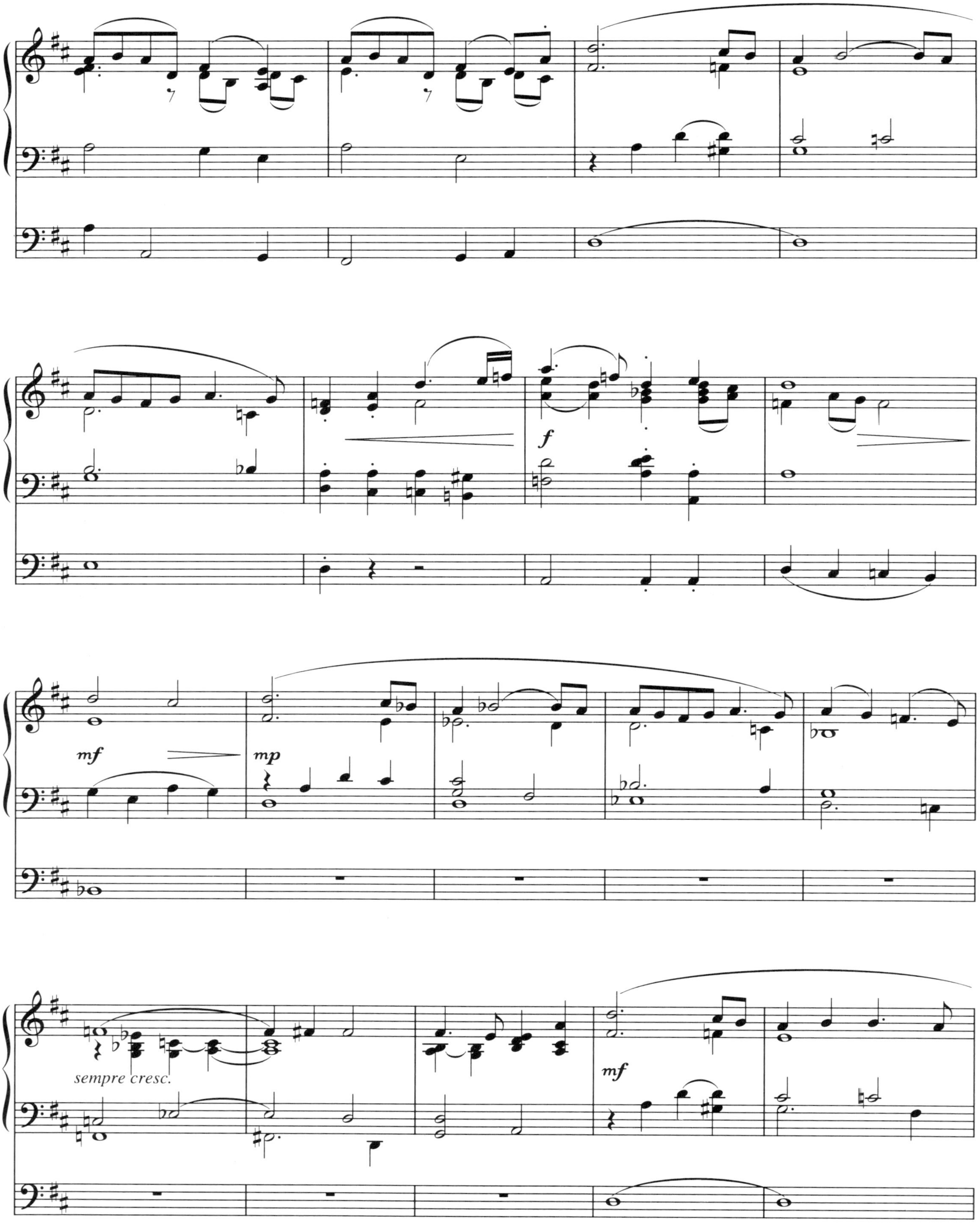
f
mf
mp
sempre cresc.
mf

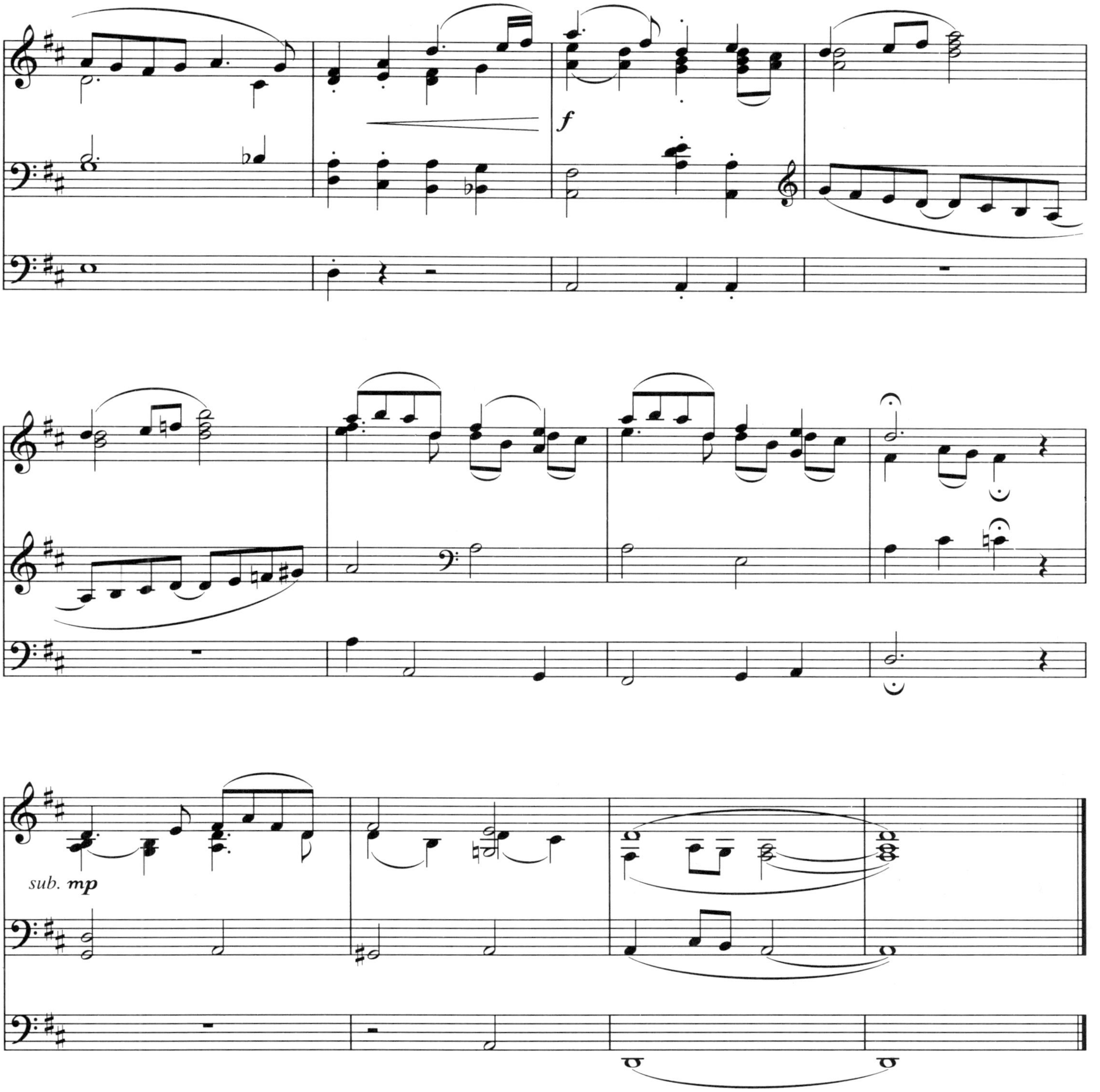
f
sub. mp

GOSPEL FANFARE

Andrew Fletcher

Allegro festivo e marcato

allargando al fine

'MARY' – 'RABBONI!'

Rosalie Bonighton

a tempo
Gt.
quasi arioso
Sw.
Sw.
+ Sw. to Gt.
quasi recit.
Gt. mf
3
poco meno mosso
Sw. p
a tempo
rit.
Sw.

a tempo
Gt. mp quasi arioso
- Sw. to Gt.
p
Sw.
poco rit.
3
3
Joyfully
a tempo
Gt. + 4'
meno mosso
Sw. p quasi recit.
Gt. f
Sw. + 4', 2'
Sw. mf
3
5
Sw. - 2'
marcato quasi recit.
Gt. f

mp
Add to Sw.
marcato
Sw. mf
poco stringendo
Add to Sw.
poco f
Sw.
poco rit.
a tempo
Gt. mp
Reduce Sw. + Gt.
Sw. p
Sw. p
molto rall.

EXULTATION

Richard Lloyd

Sw. to Mixture, Reed 8'
Gt. Fifteenth + Sw. to Gt.

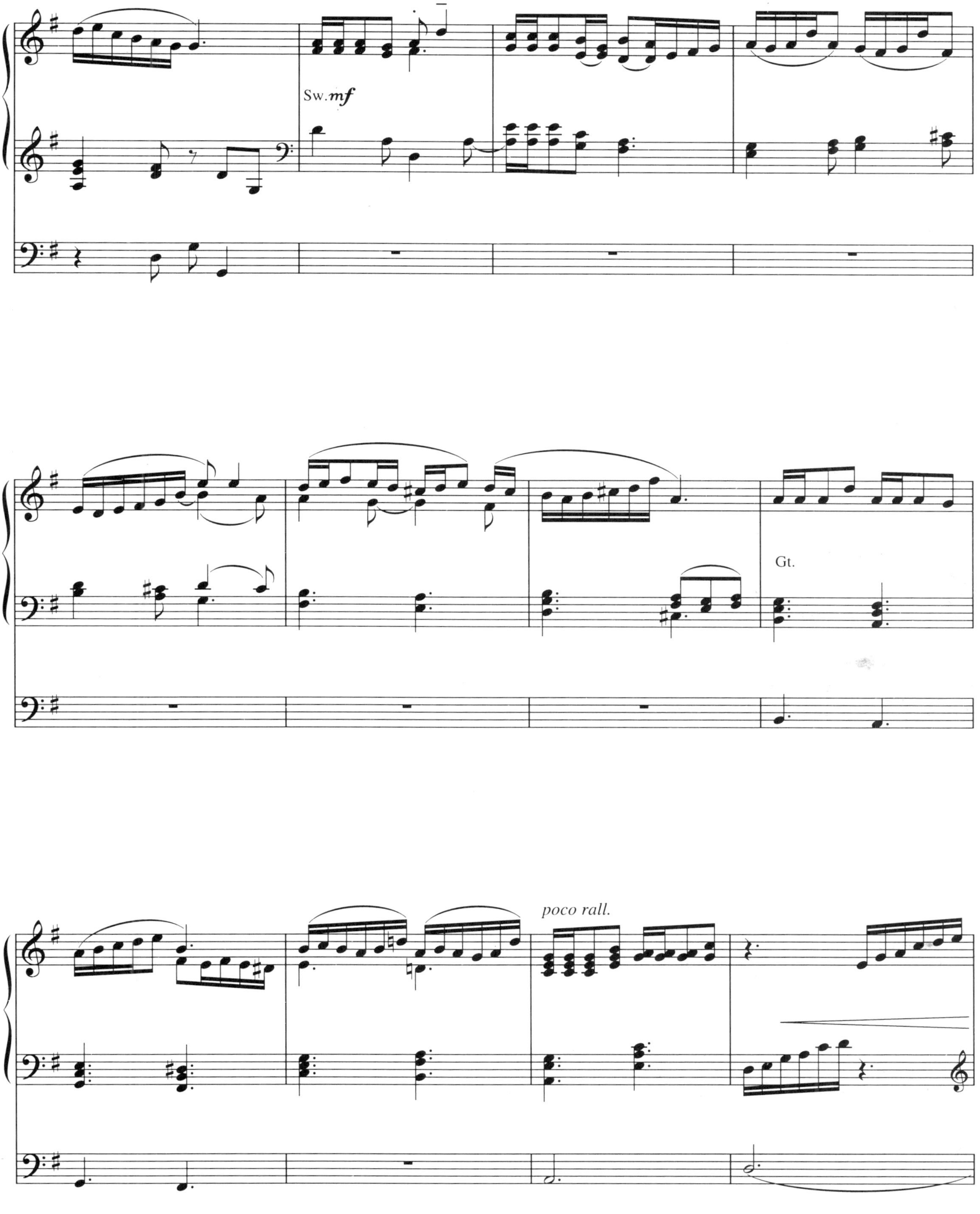
Sw. mf
Gt.
poco rall.

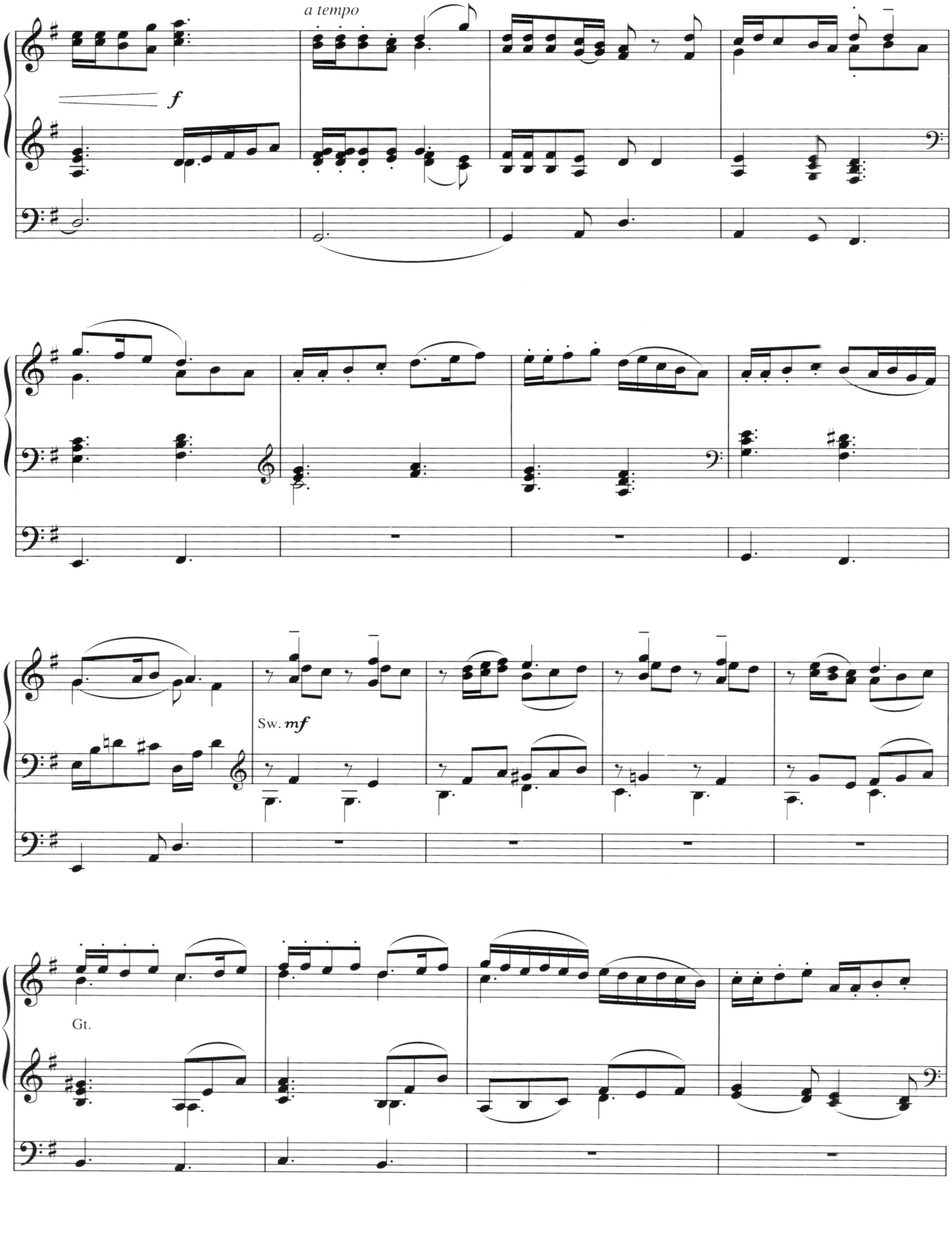
a tempo
f
Sw. mf
Gt.

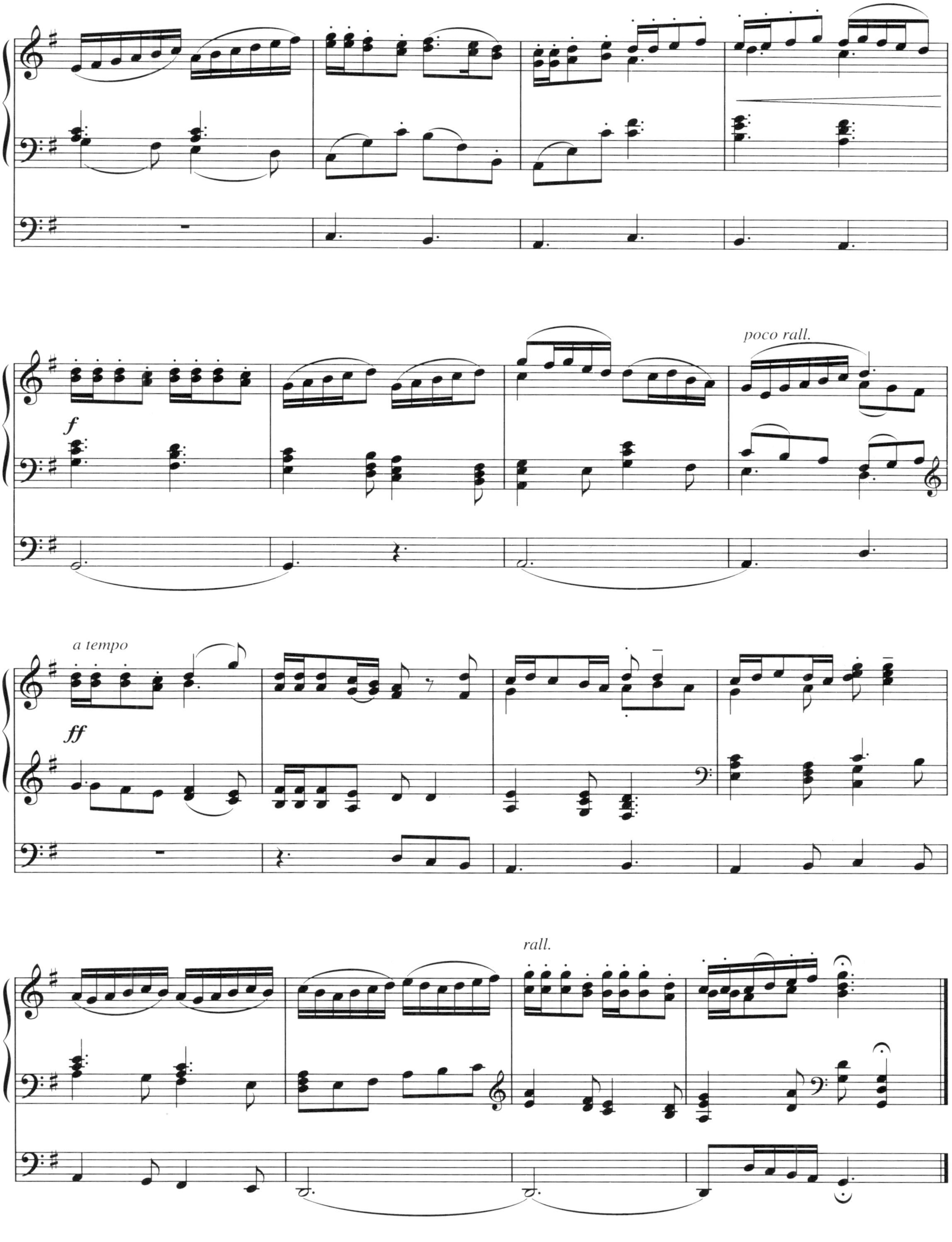
f
poco rall.
a tempo
ff
rall.

EASTER ALLELUIAS

Martin Setchell

Sw. Reeds
Gt. to Mixtures
Ped. 16', 8'

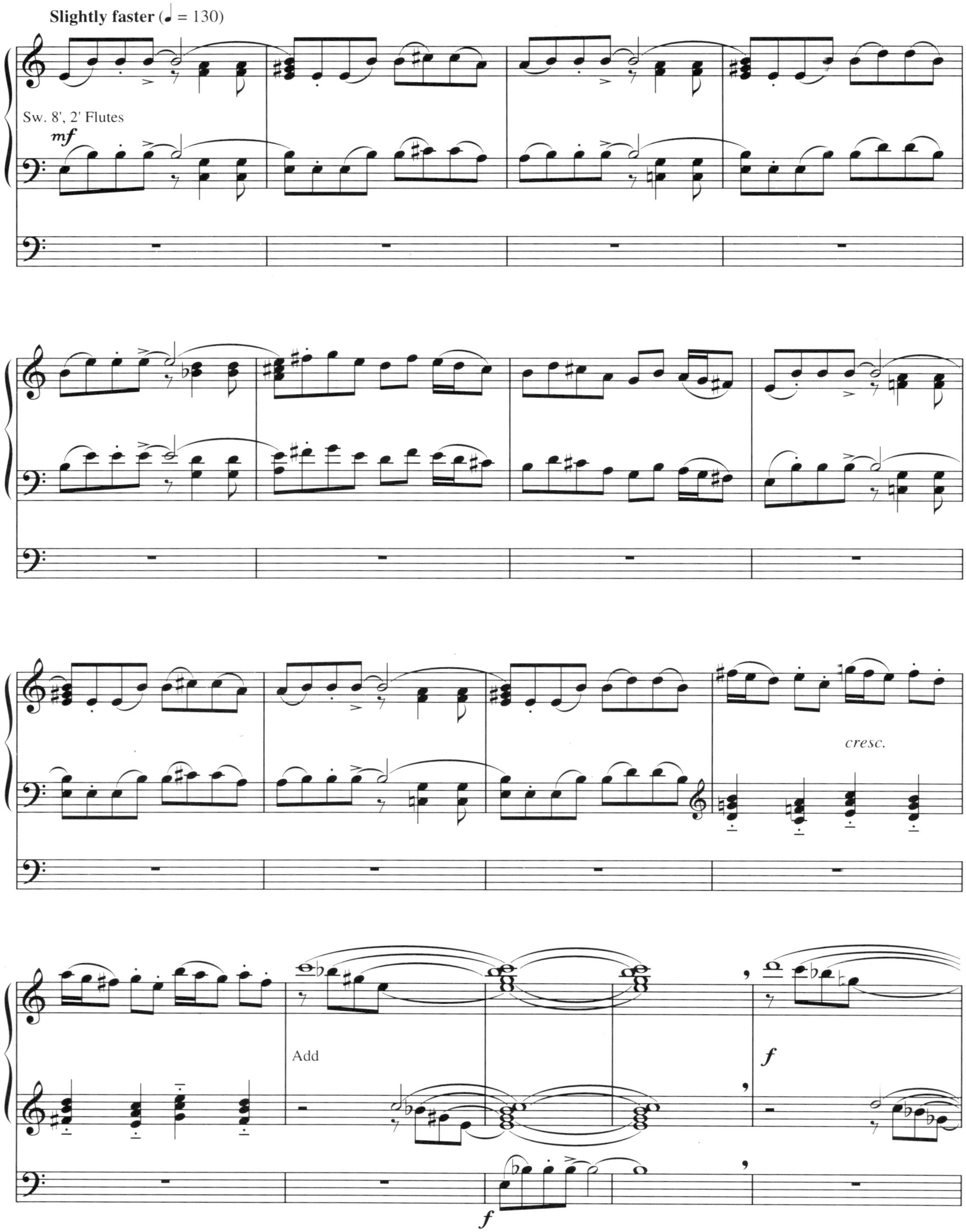
Slightly faster (♩ = 130)
Sw. 8', 2' Flutes
mf
cresc.
Add
f
f

allargando
Gt.
Tempo I
Solo Tpt.
or Tuba 8'
ff
Gt.
Solo Tuba
Gt.
Grandioso
tutti forza
ffff

CHRIST TRIUMPHANT

John Marsh

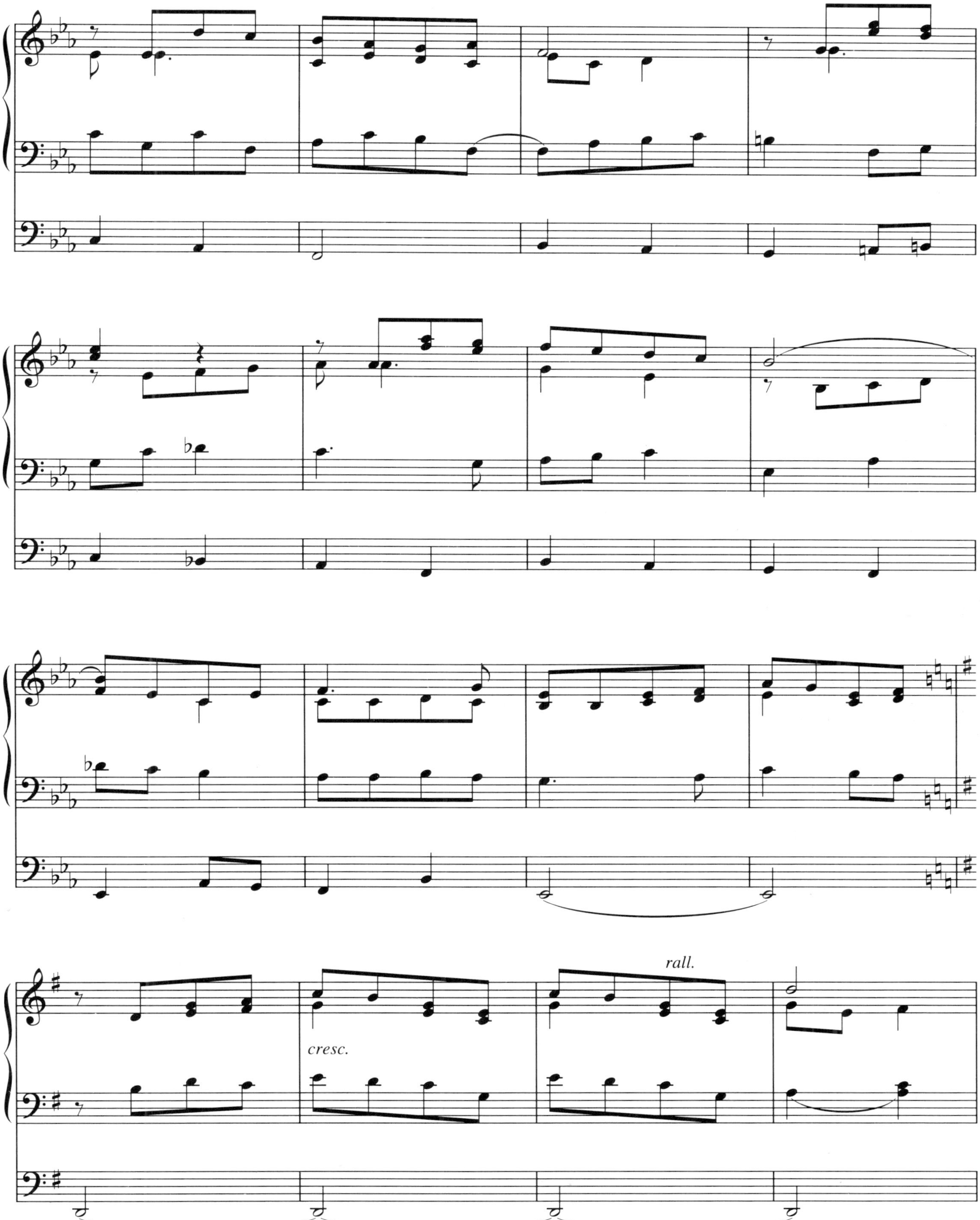
cresc.
rall.

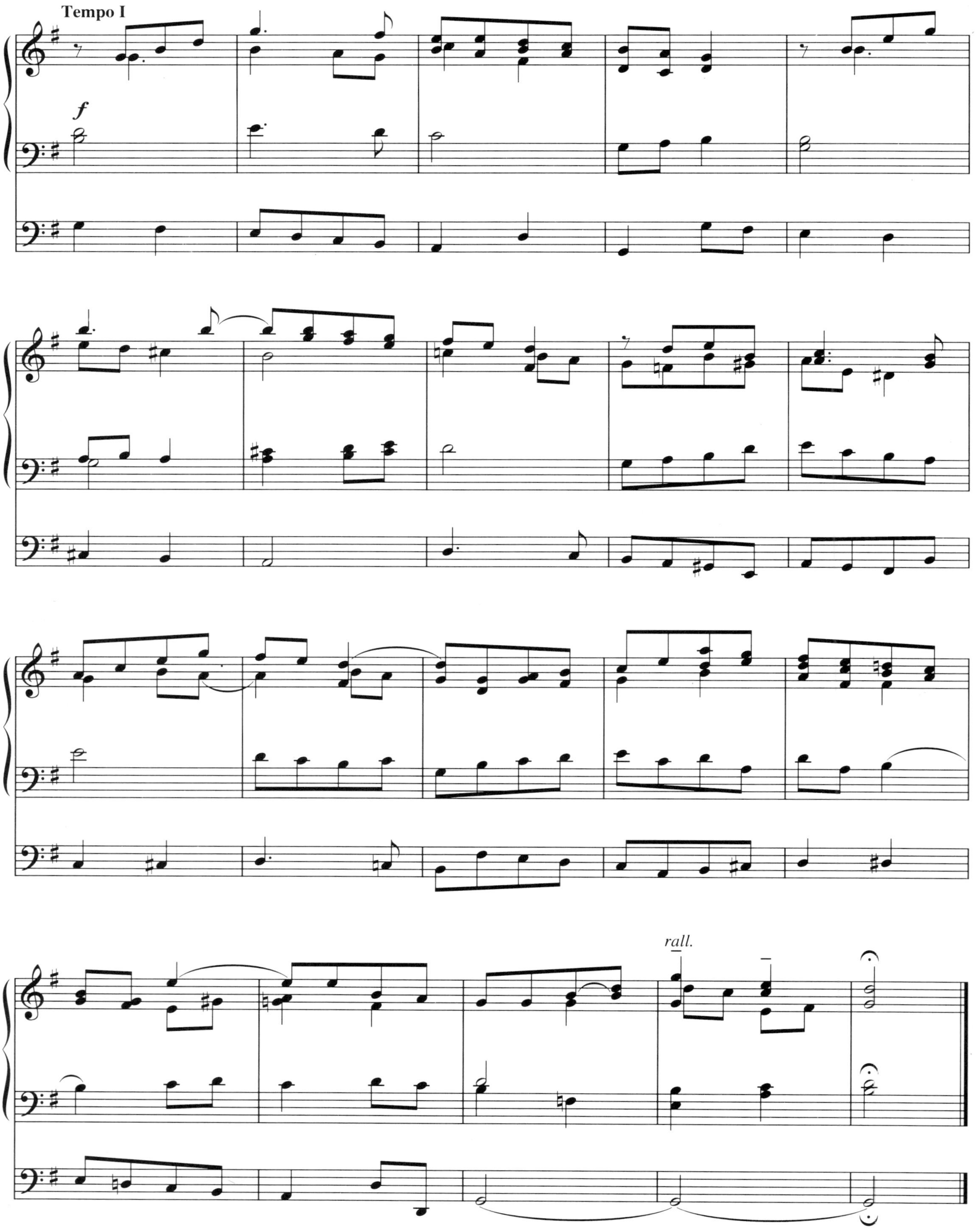
Tempo I
f
rall.

HOLY, HOLY, HOLY

Malcolm McKelvey

Sw. to Mixture
Gt. Trumpet
Ped. 16', 8' + Sw. to Ped.

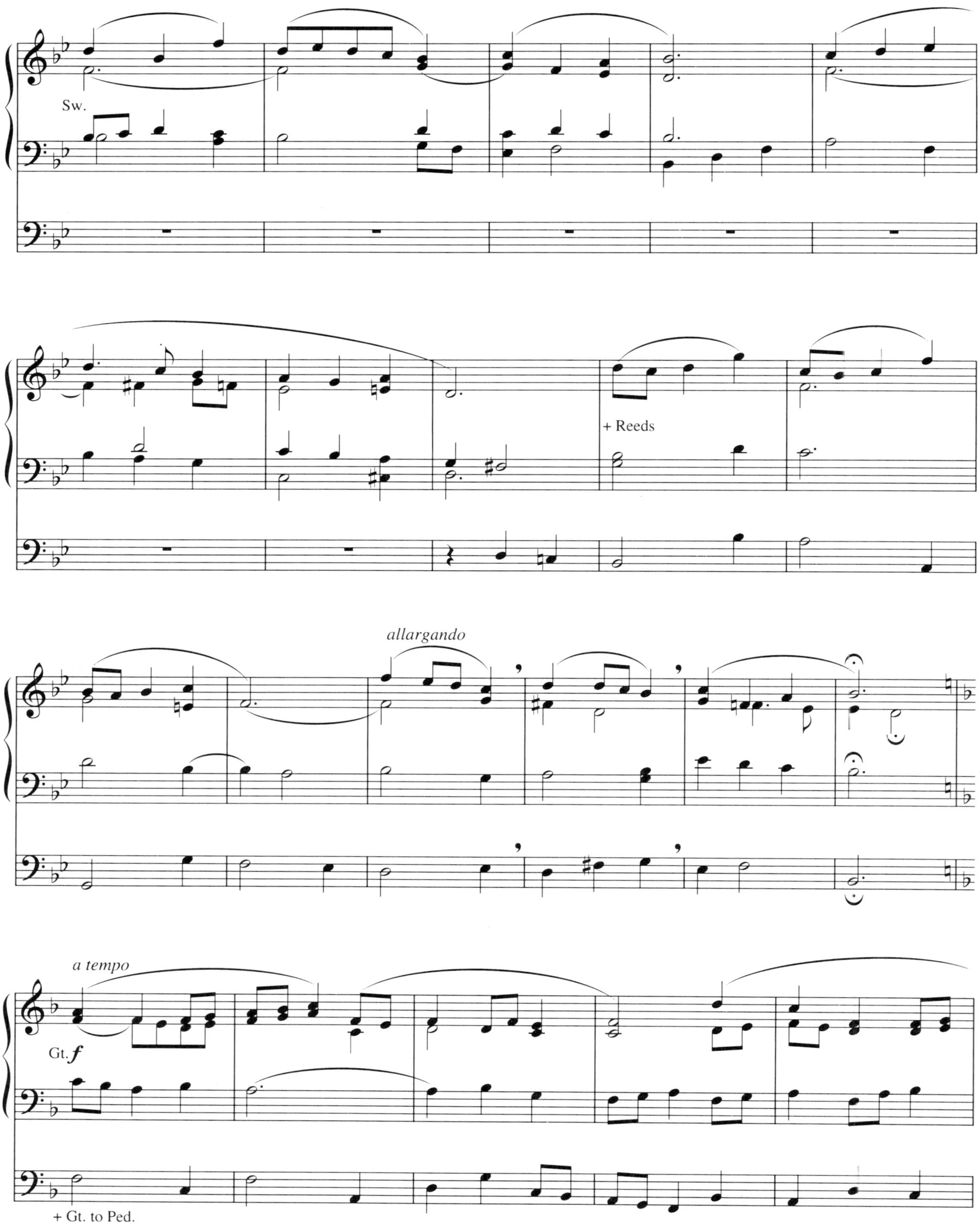
Sw.
+ Reeds
allargando
a tempo
Gt. f
+ Gt. to Ped.

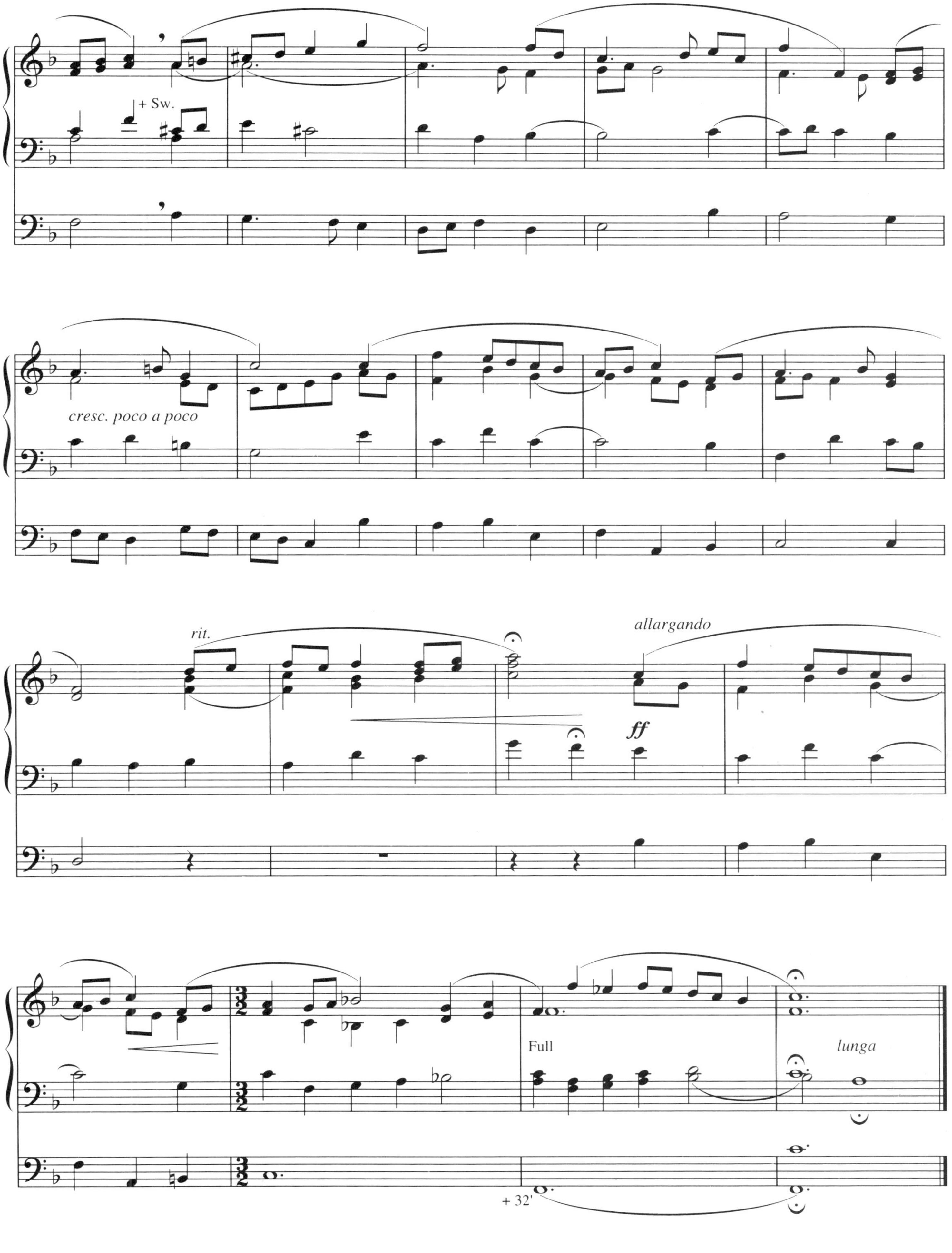
+ Sw.
cresc. poco a poco
rit.
allargando
ff
Full
lunga
+ 32'

REFLECTION ON 'ADORO TE DEVOTE'

Andrew Moore

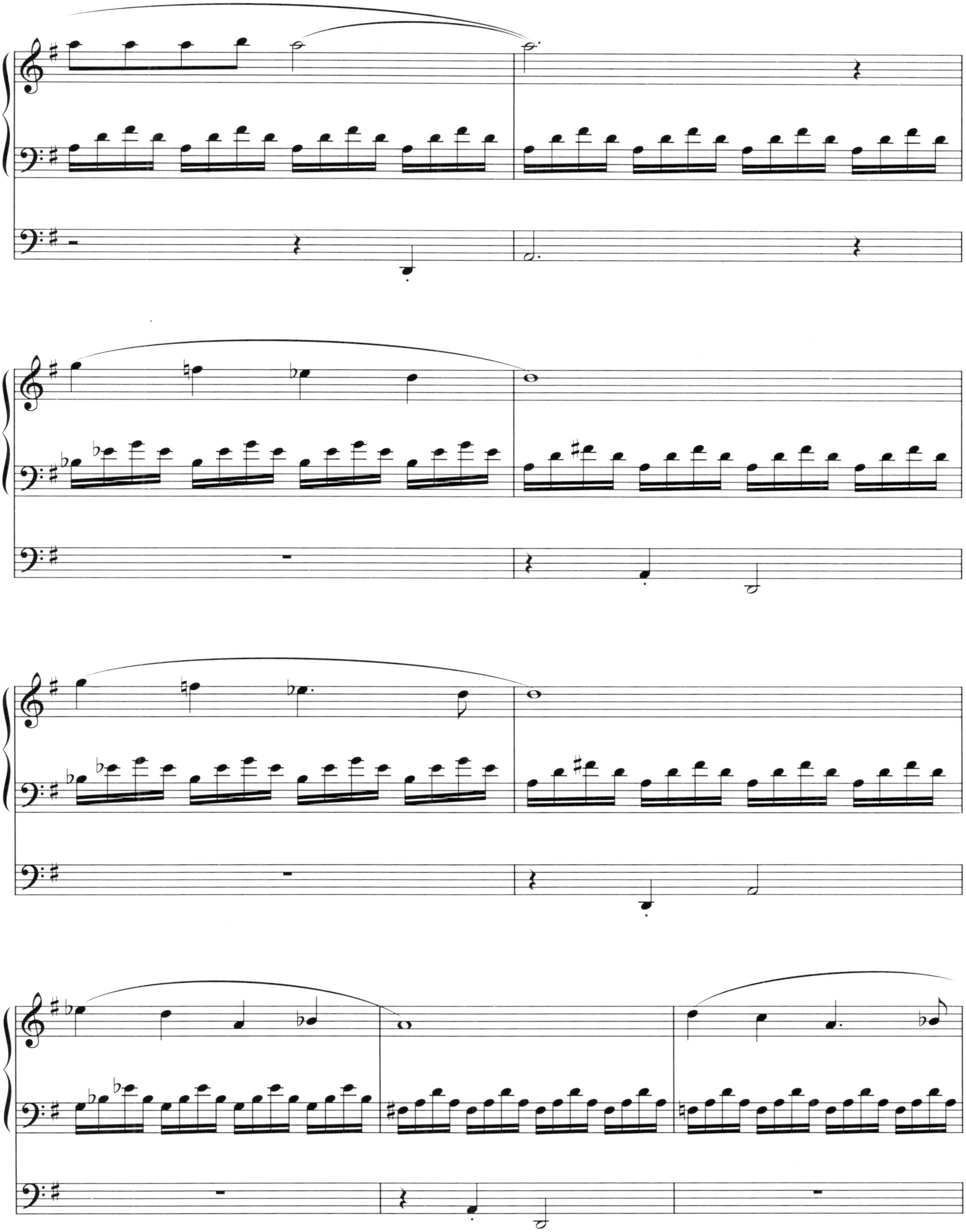

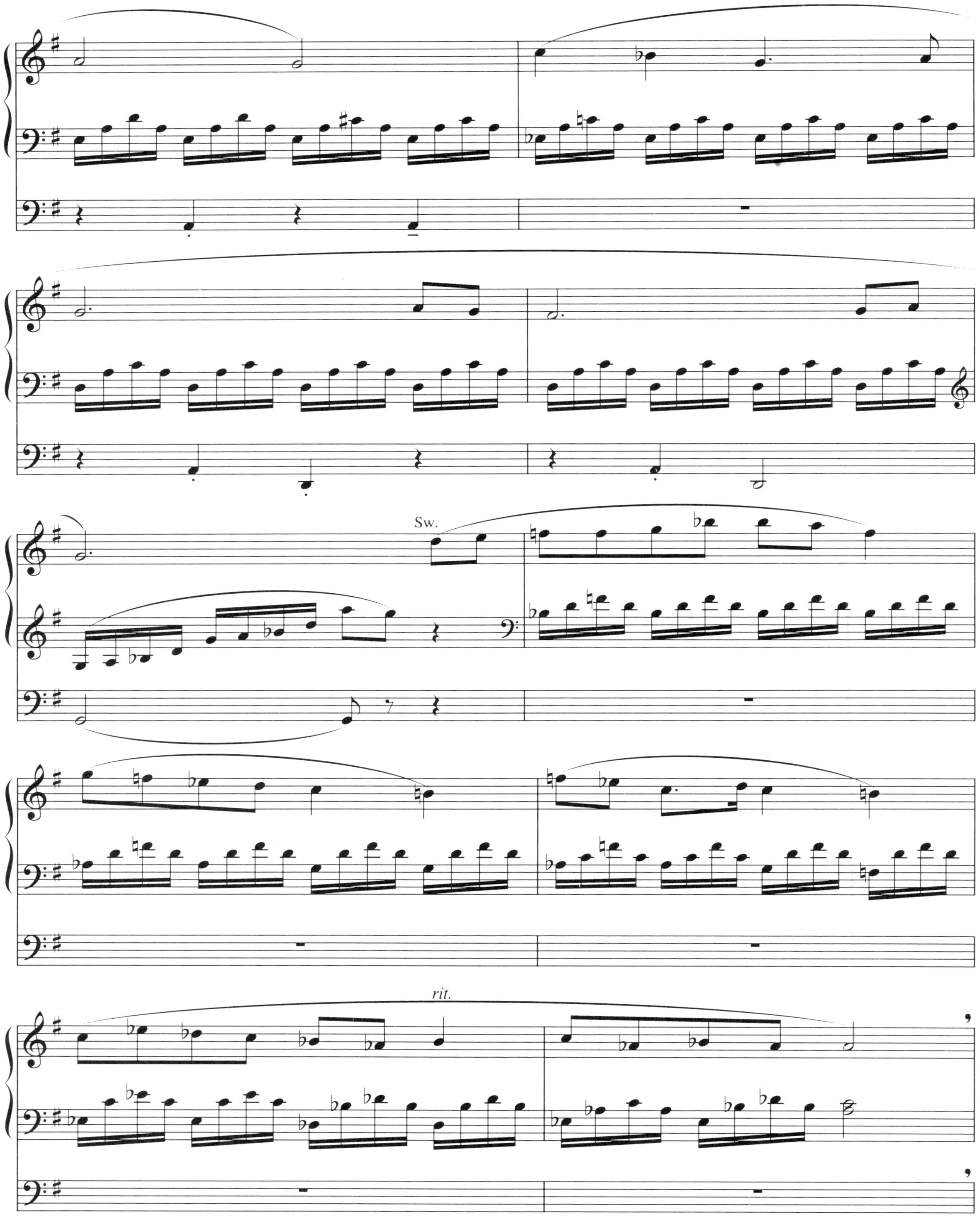
Sw.
rit.

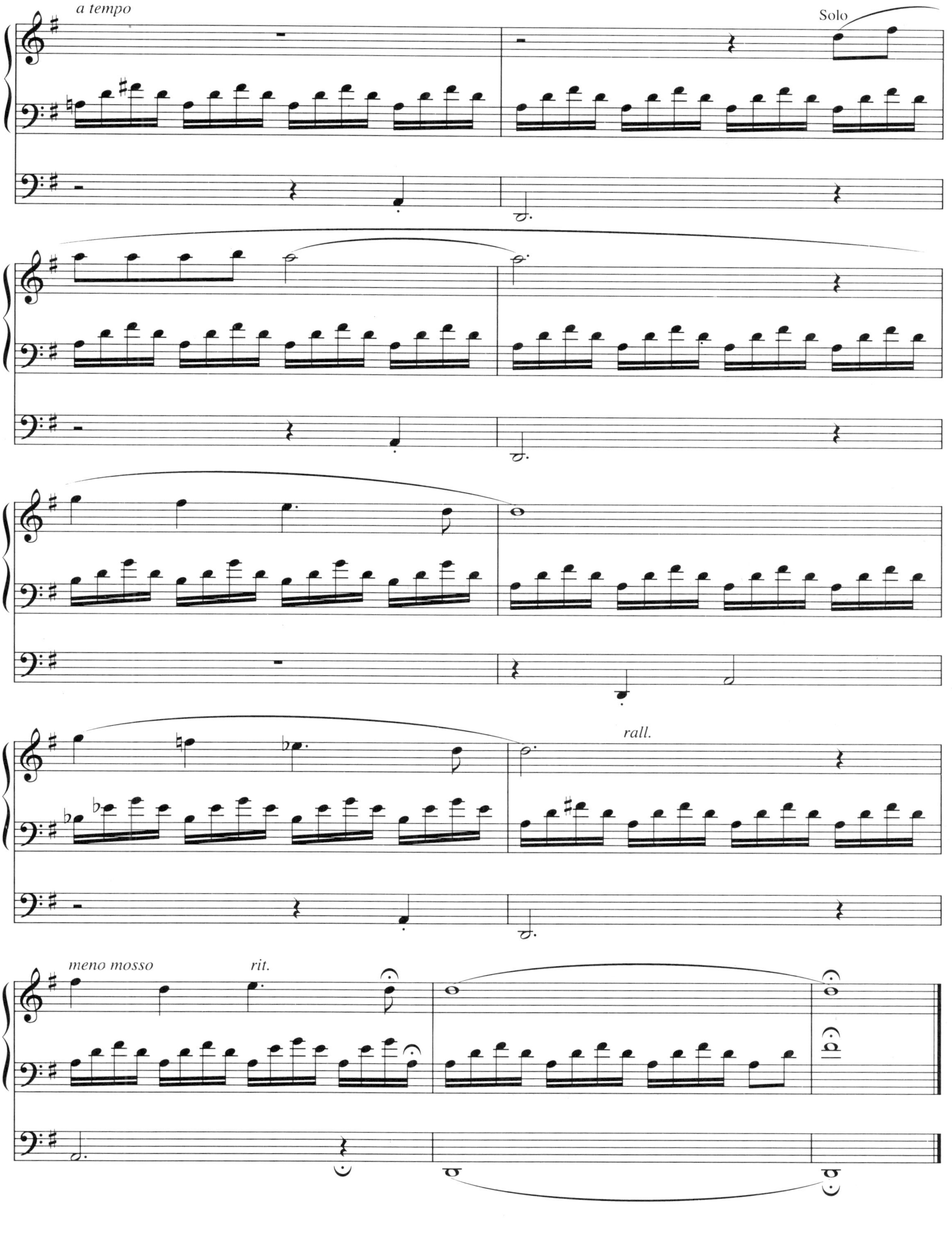
a tempo
Solo
rall.
meno mosso
rit.

PRELUDE ON 'VENI SANCTE SPIRITUS'

Colin Mawby

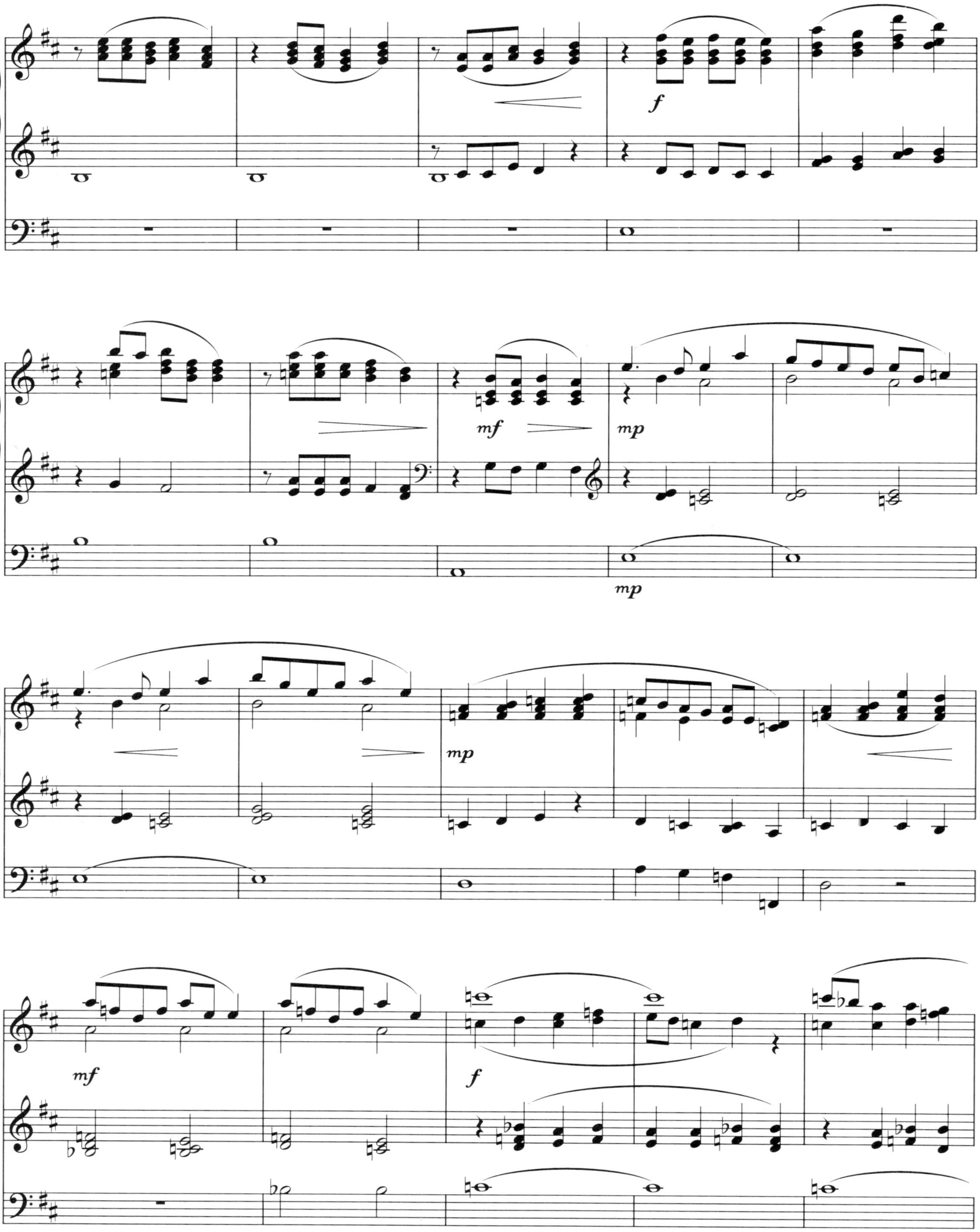
f
mf
mp
mp
mp
mf
f

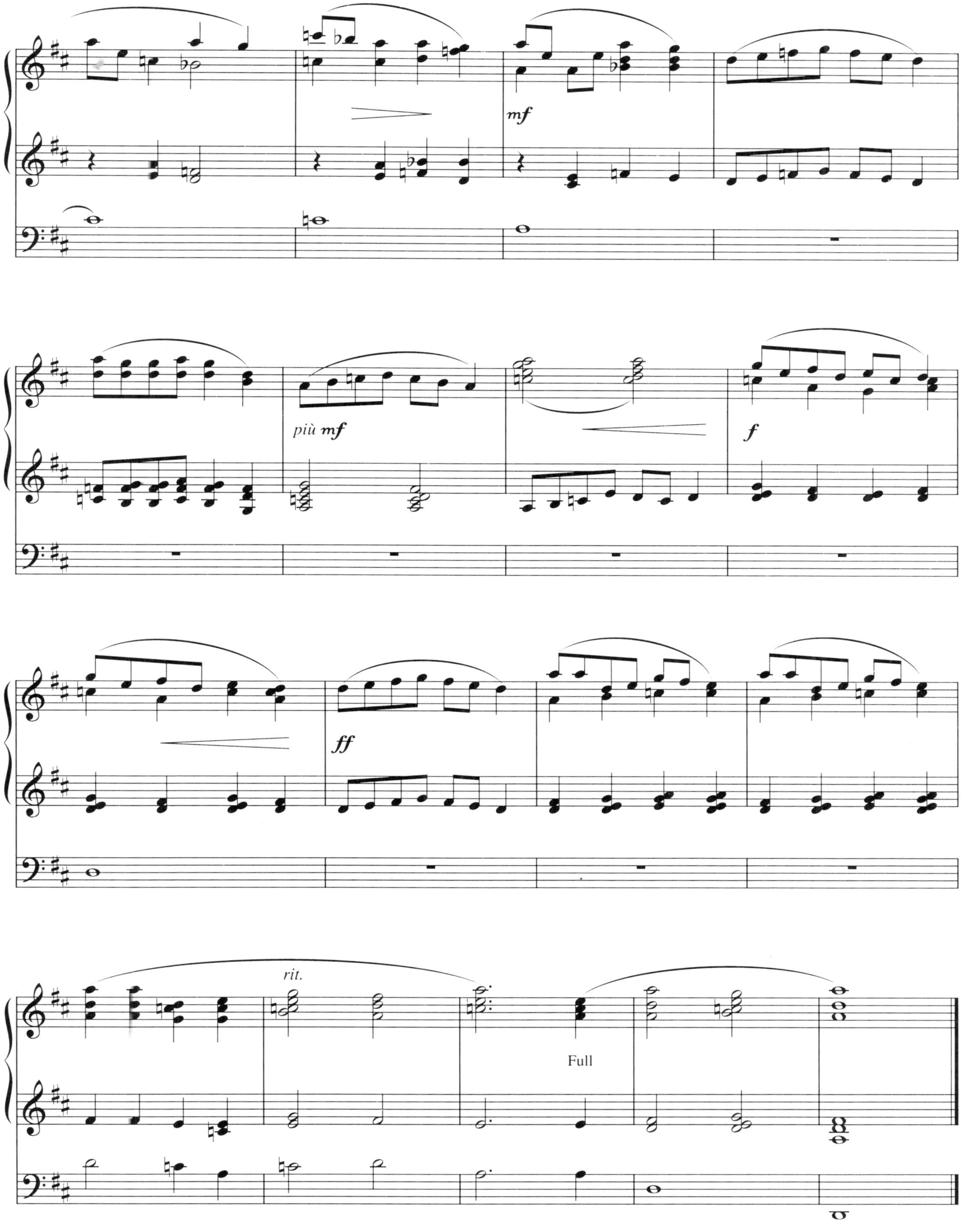
mf
più mf
f
ff
rit.
Full

ORDINARY TIME – MORE OR LESS

Rosalie Bonighton

(2nd time - Gt. to Ped.)   Sw. to Ped.

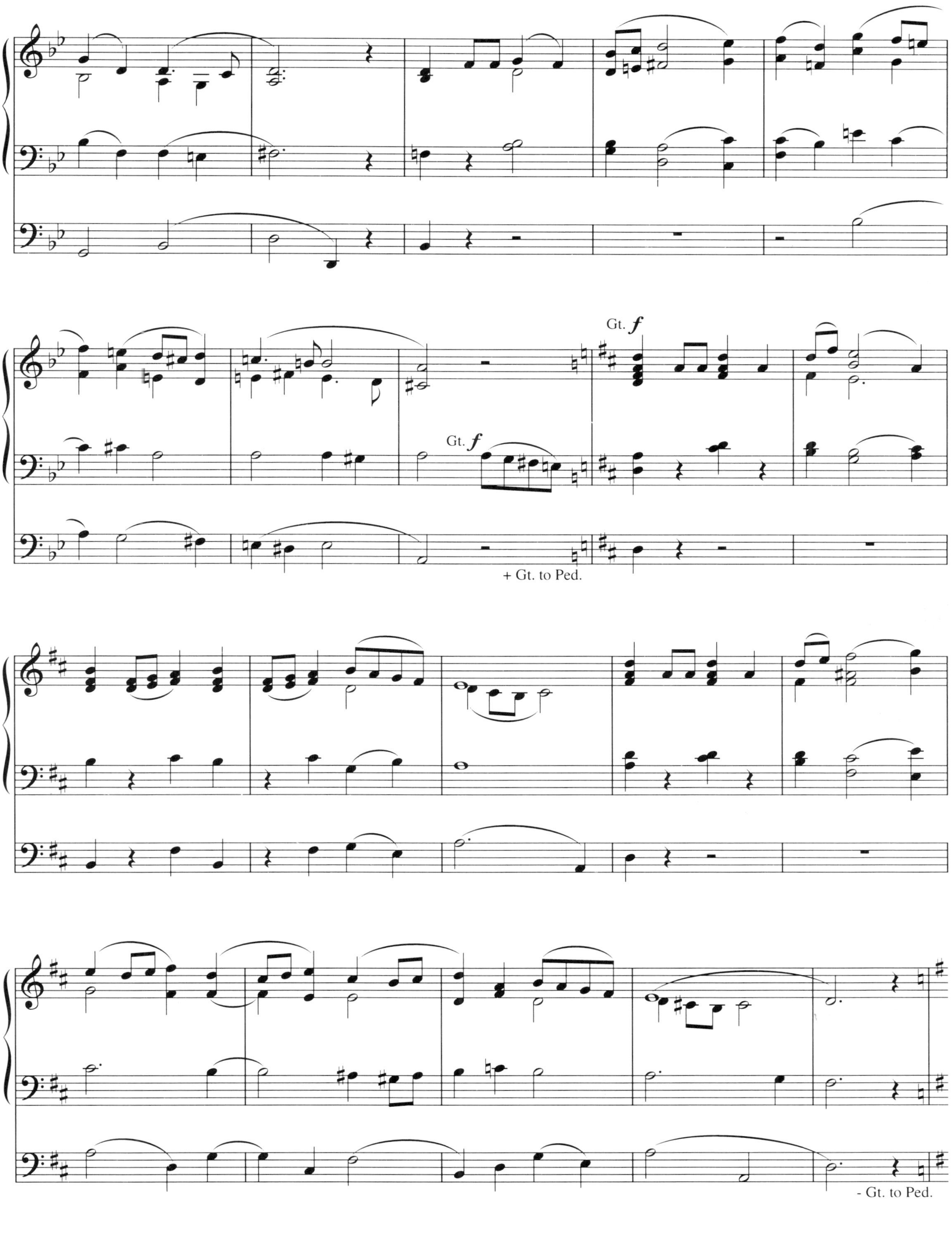
Gt. f
Gt. f
+ Gt. to Ped.
- Gt. to Ped.

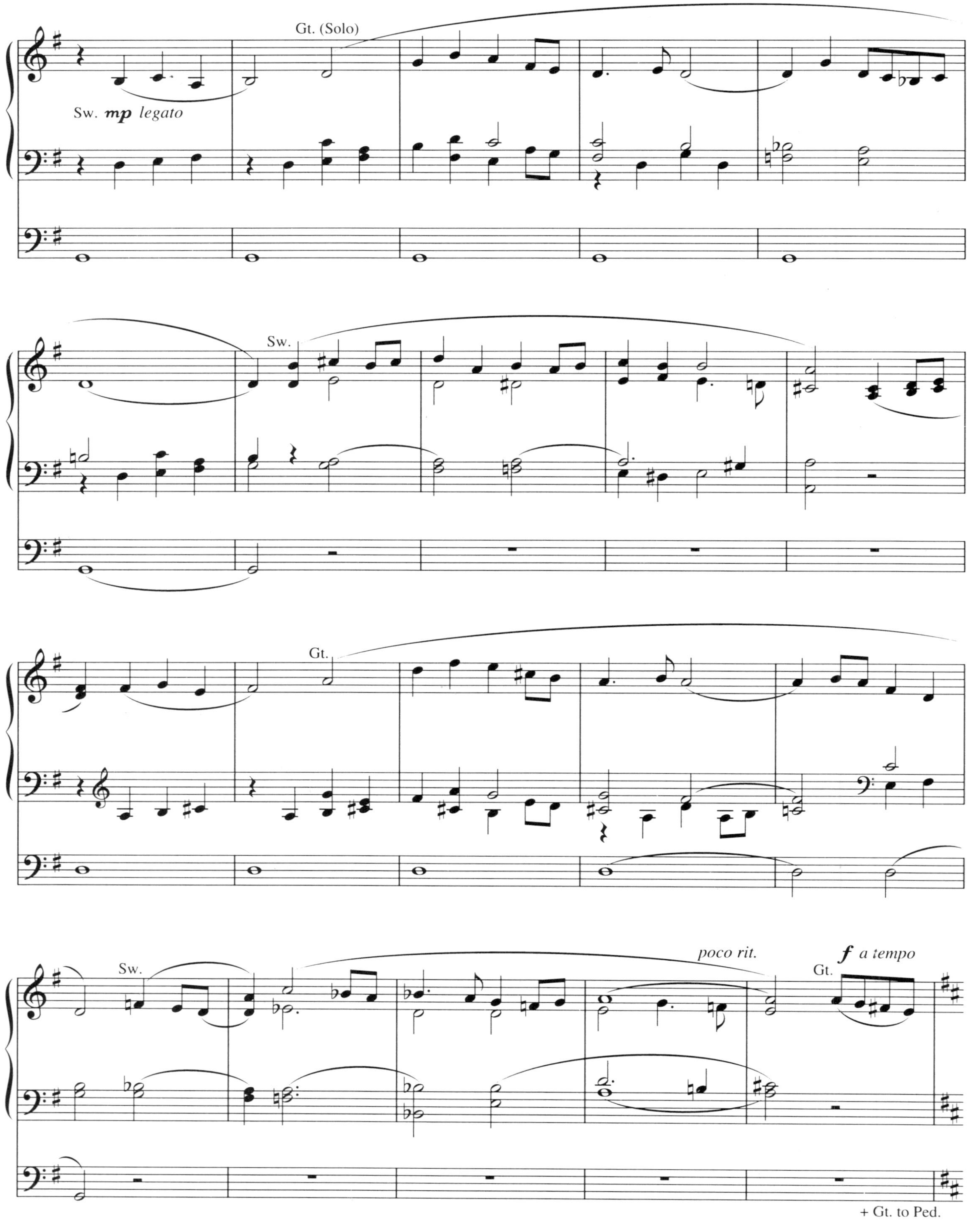
Gt. (Solo)
Sw. mp legato
Sw.
Gt.
Sw.
poco rit.
f a tempo
Gt.
+ Gt. to Ped.

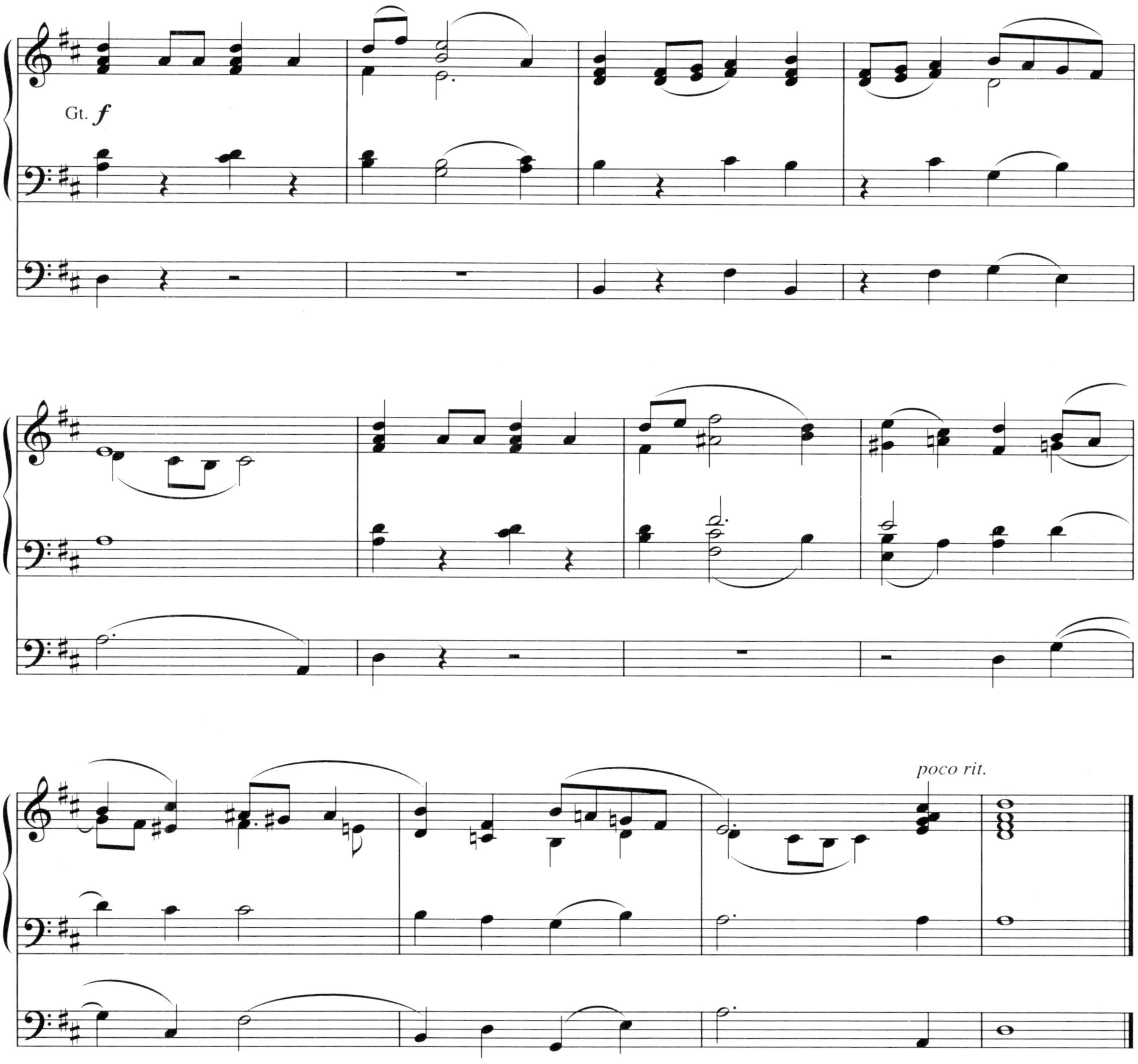
Gt. *f*
poco rit.

CANTILENA

Stanley Vann

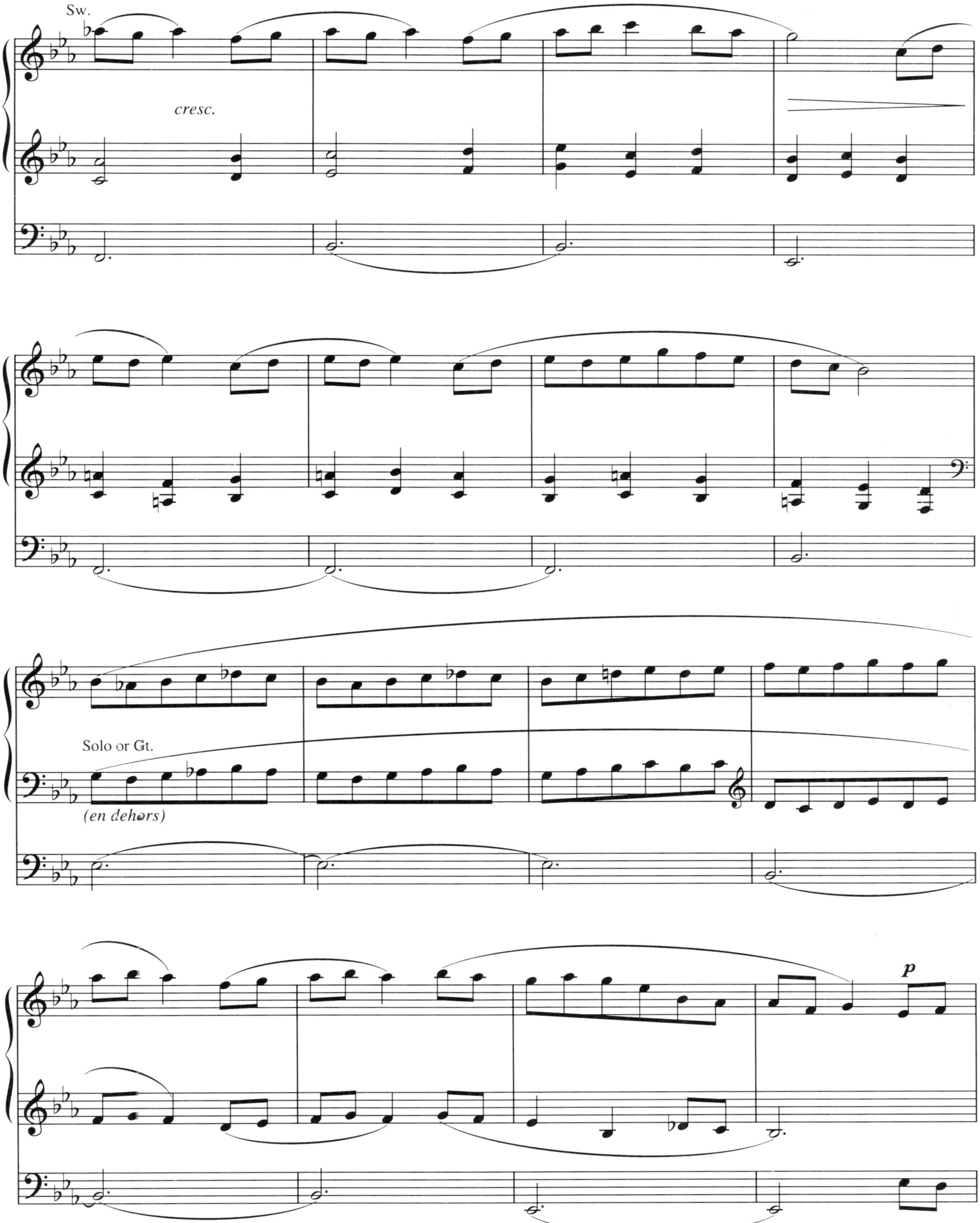
Sw.
cresc.
Solo or Gt.
(en dehors)
p

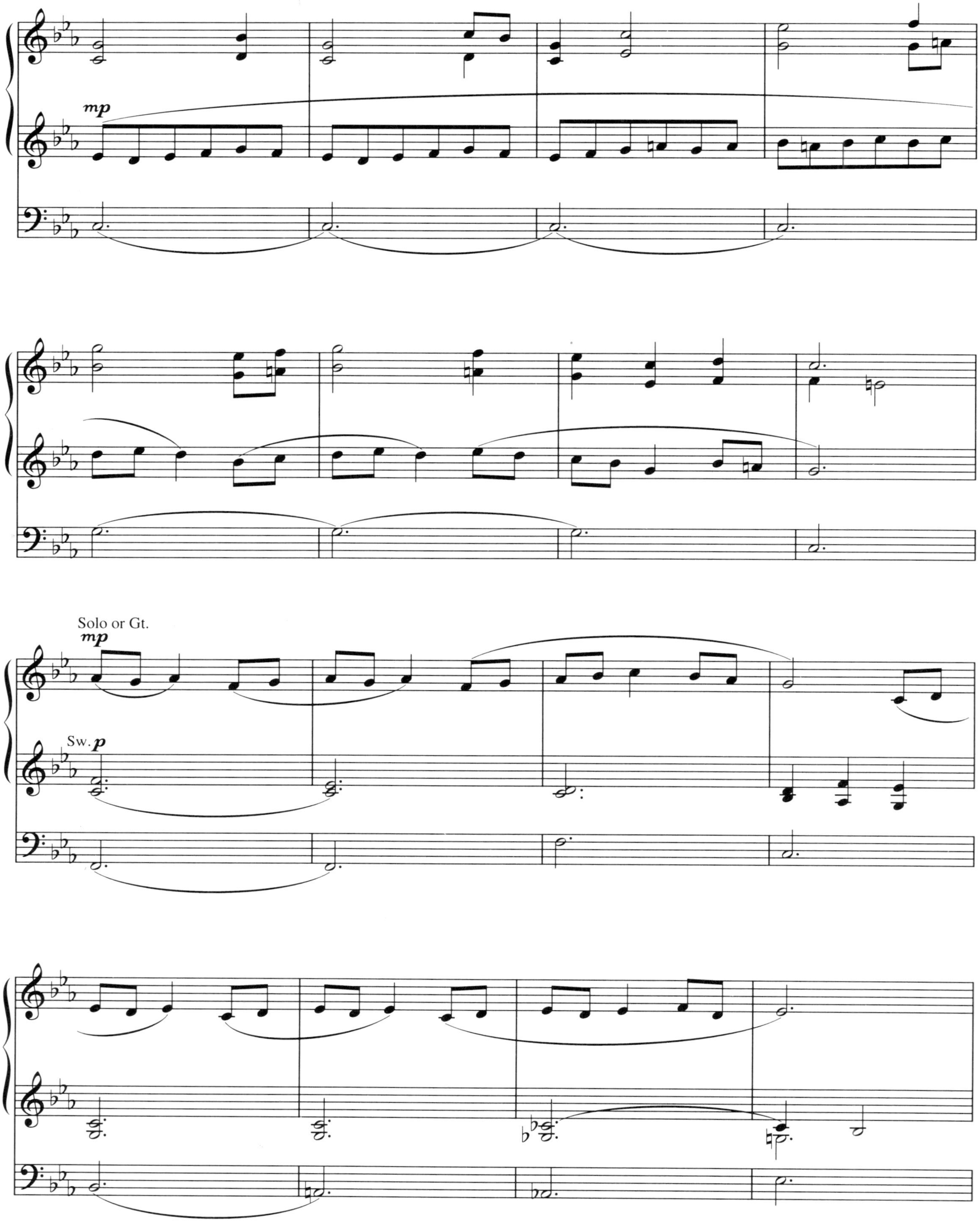
mp
Solo or Gt.
mp
Sw. p

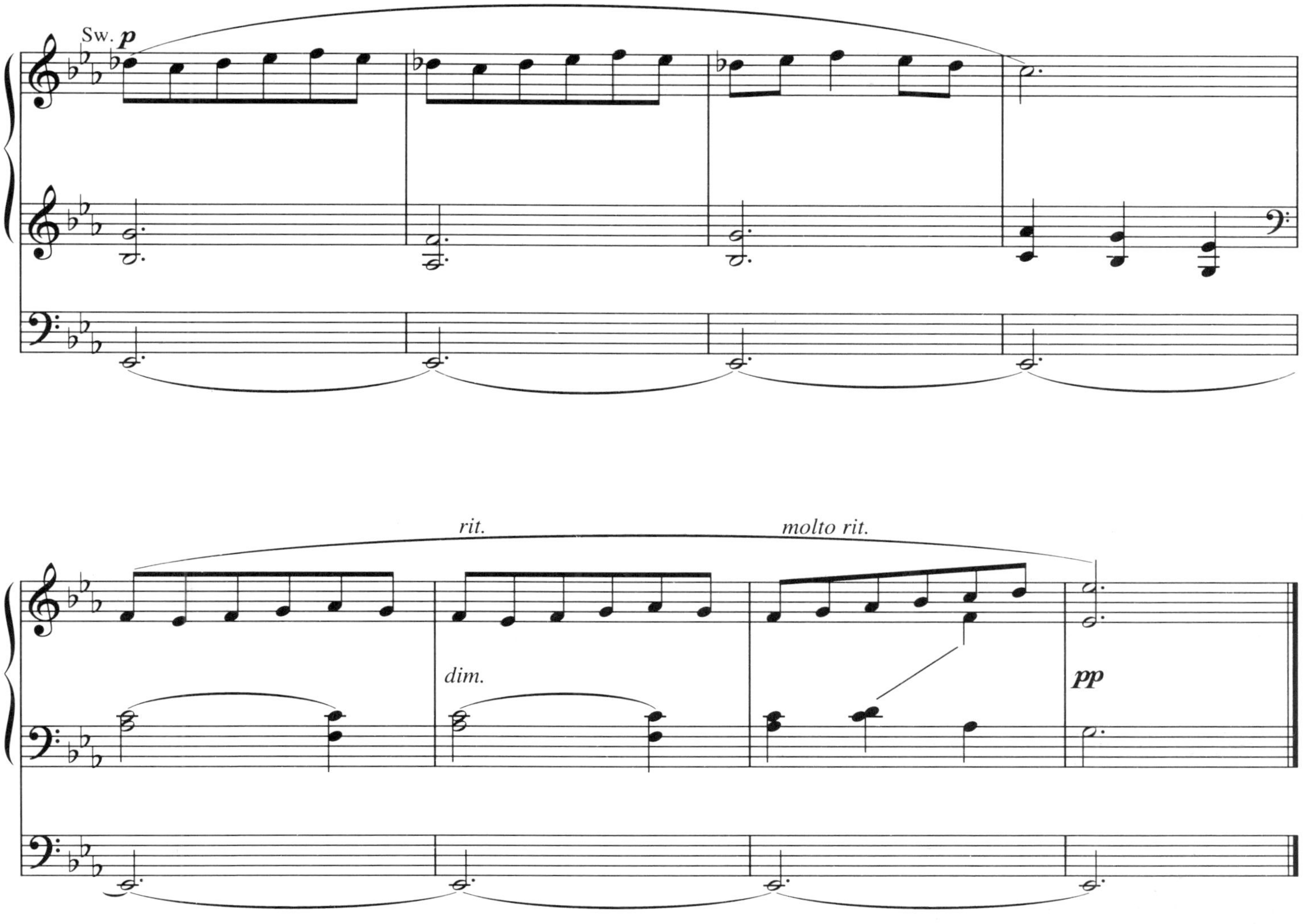
Sw. p
rit.
molto rit.
dim.
pp

PASSACAGLIA ON A DANISH THREEFOLD AMEN

Martin Setchell

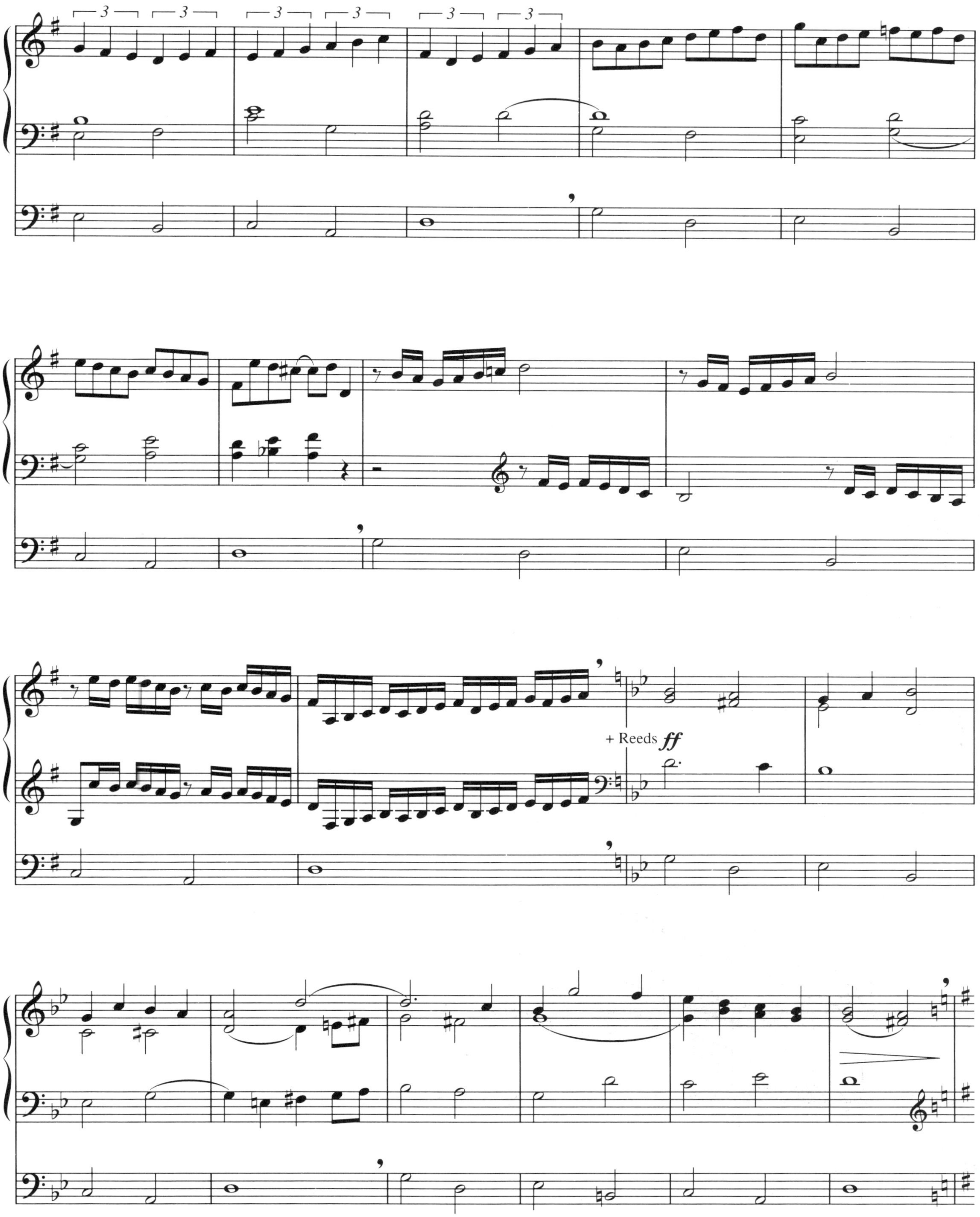

+ Reeds ff

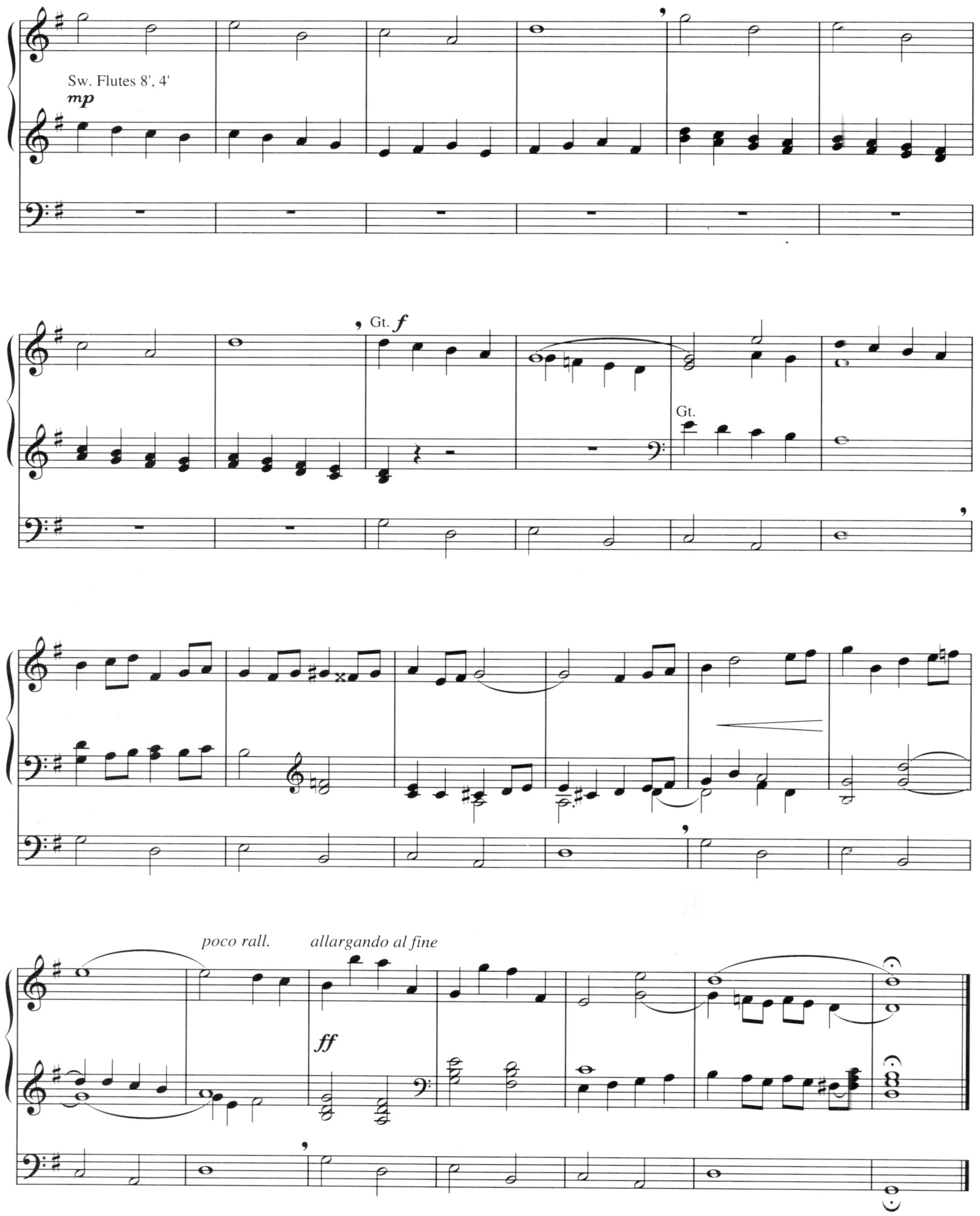
Sw. Flutes 8', 4'
mp
Gt. f
Gt.
poco rall.
allargando al fine
ff

ITE, MISSA EST

James Patten

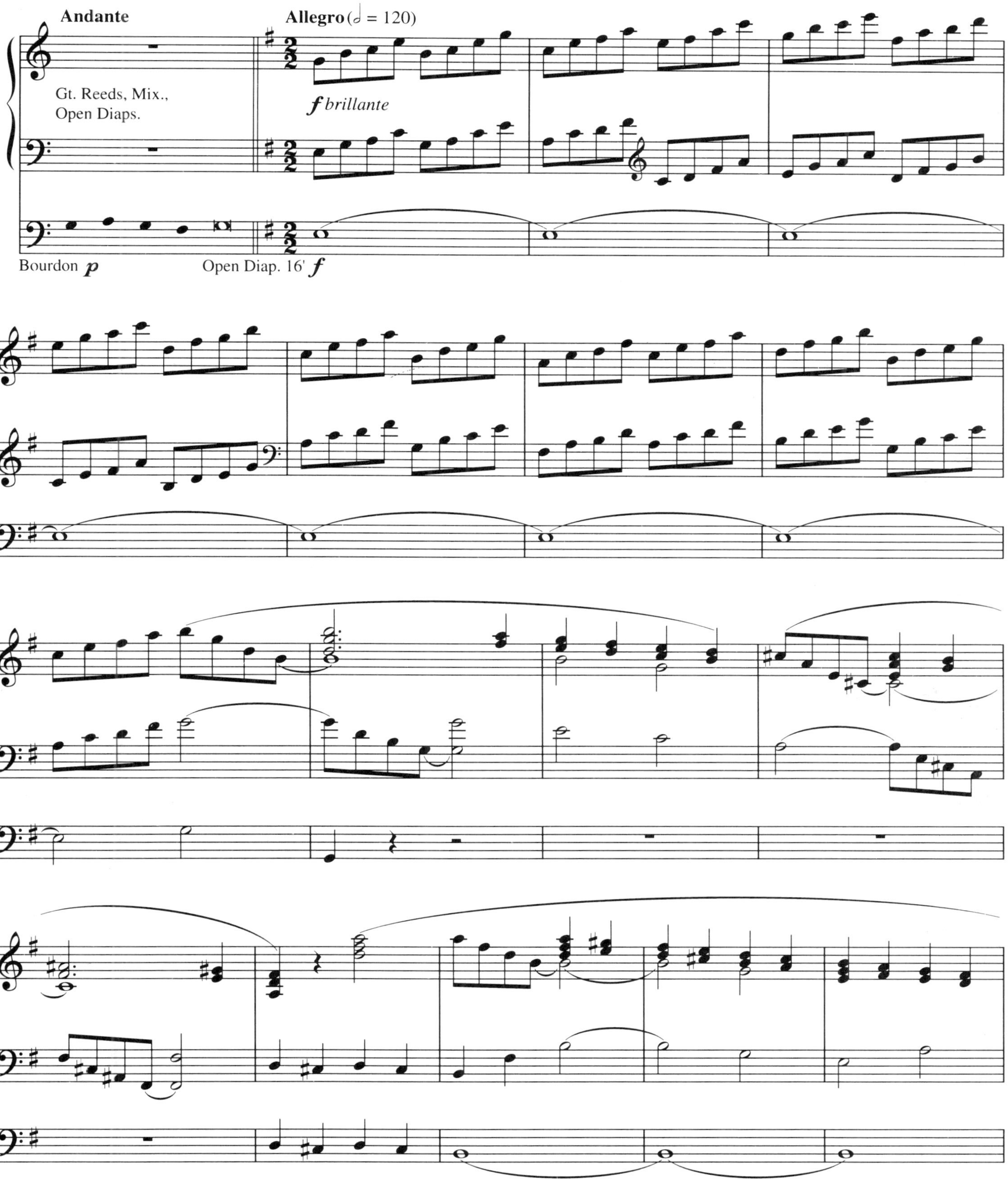

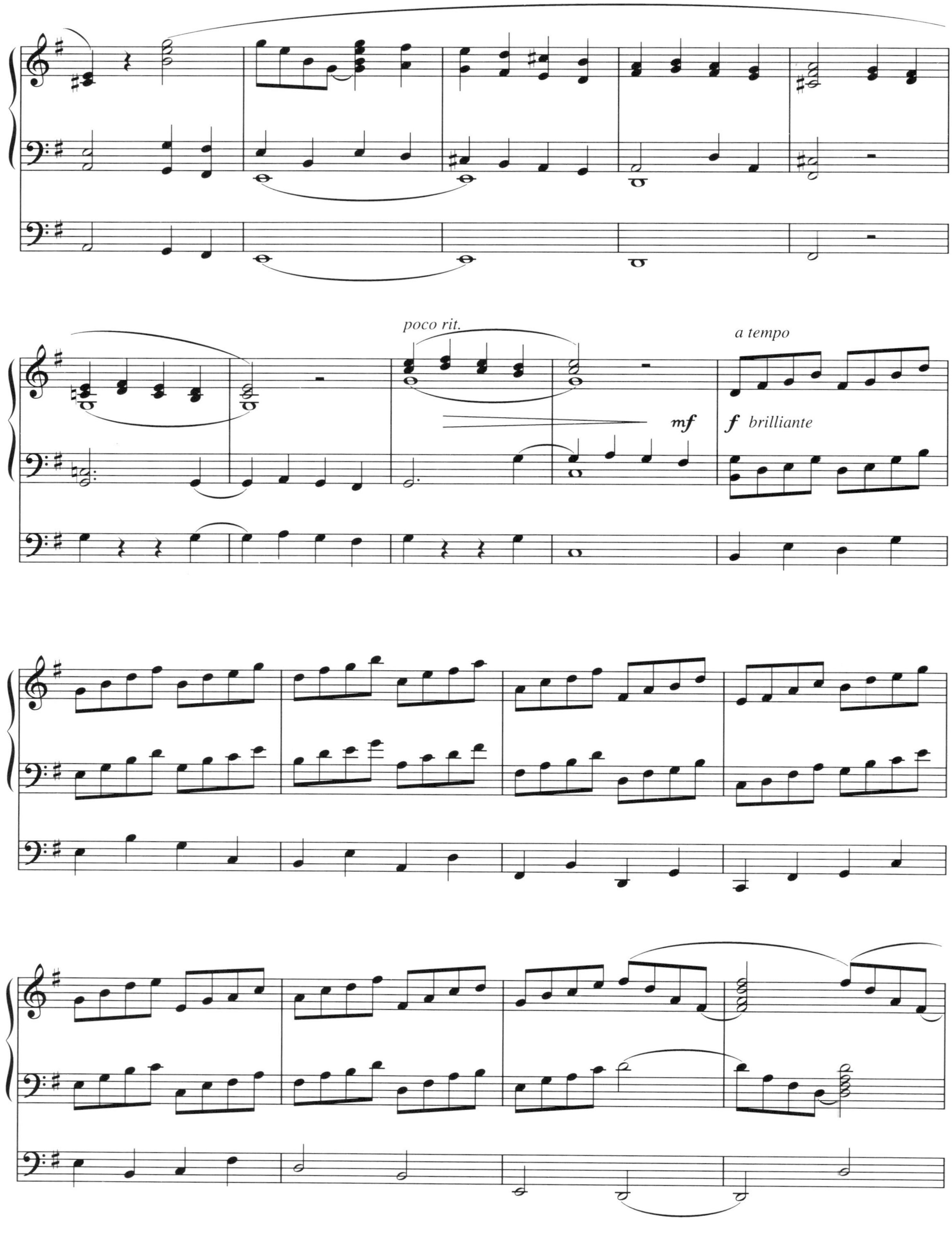
poco rit.
a tempo
mf
f brilliante

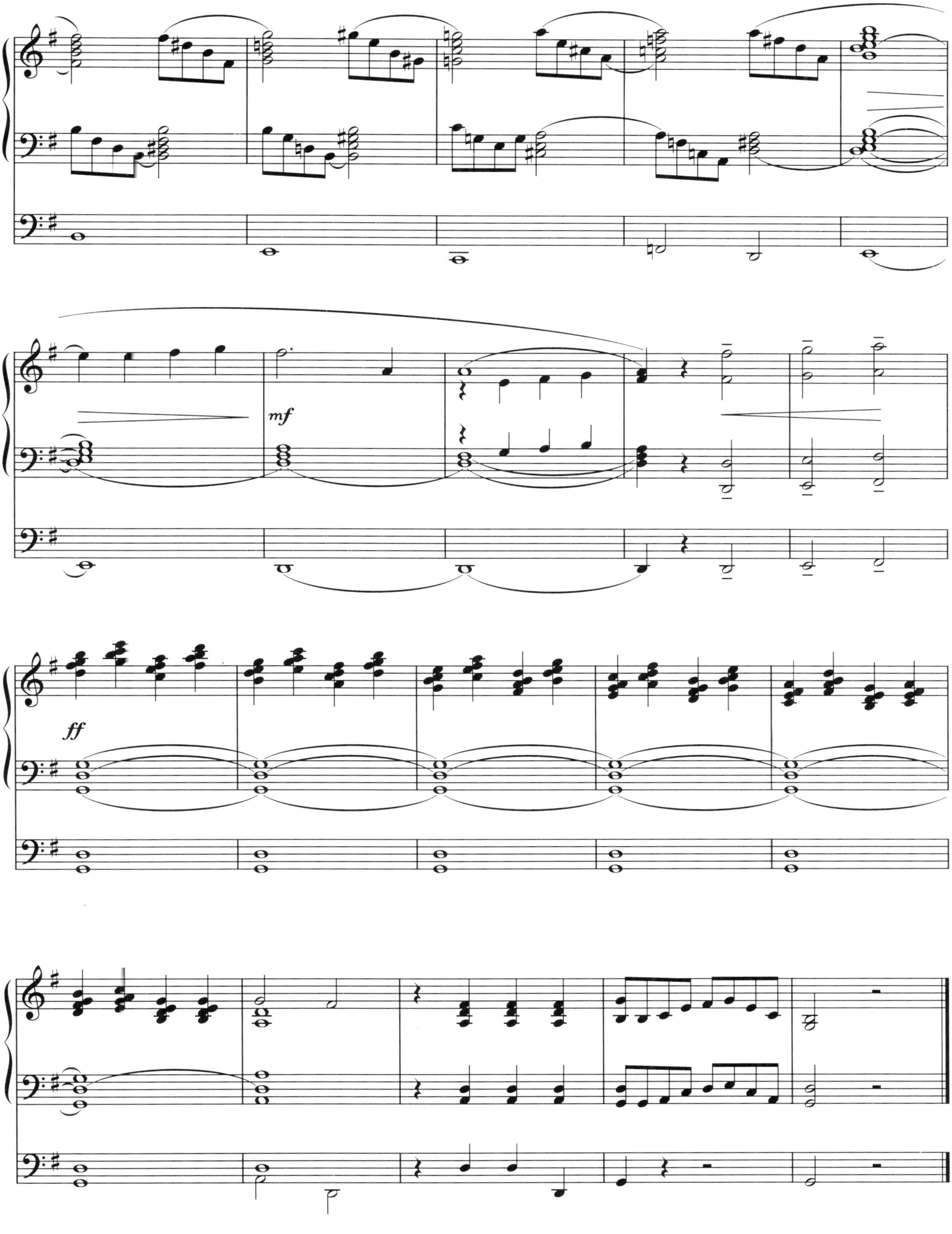
mf
ff

For Peter Gray

ST FELIX

Betty Roe

mf
Solo 8' f
rall.
meno mosso
16' + Sw. to Ped.
D.C. al Coda
CODA
meno mosso
p
pp
Fine

LITTERARUM ORDINE

Richard Proulx

Sw. Plenum + Reeds
Gt. Plenum + Reeds, Sw. to Gt.
Ped. 16', 8', 4', Sw. to Ped.

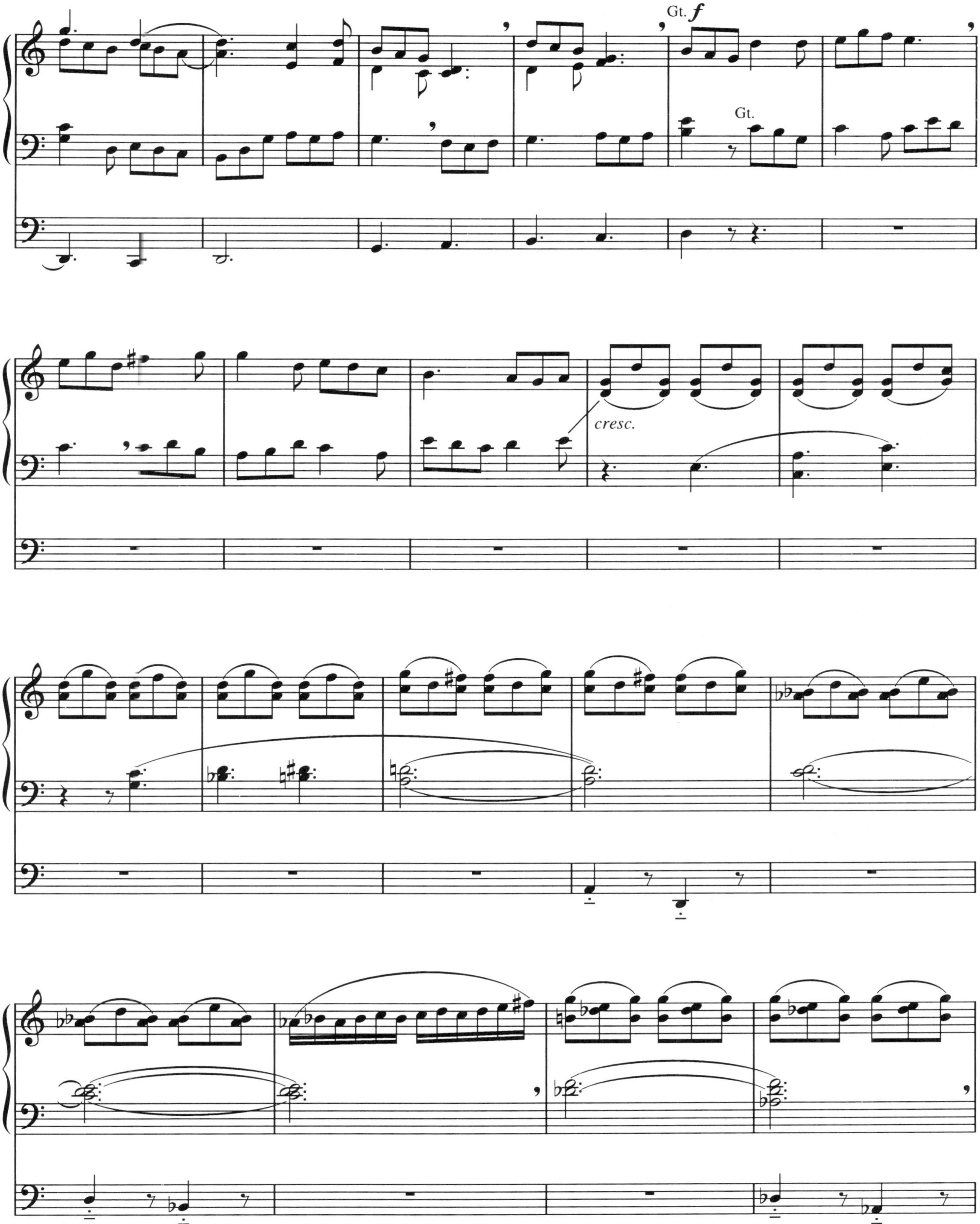
Gt. f
Gt.
cresc.

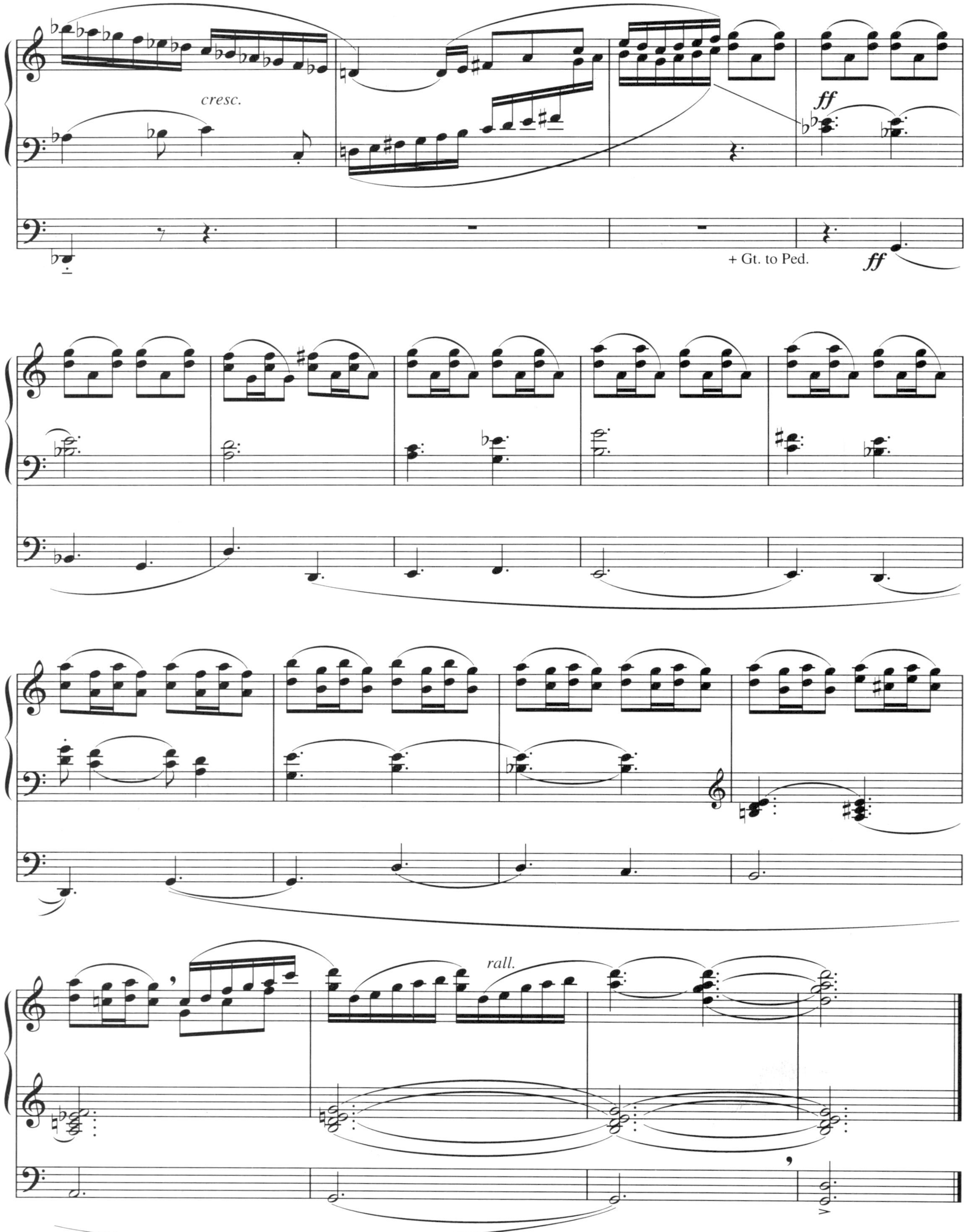
cresc.
ff
+ Gt. to Ped.
ff
rall.

ACCLAMATION

June Nixon

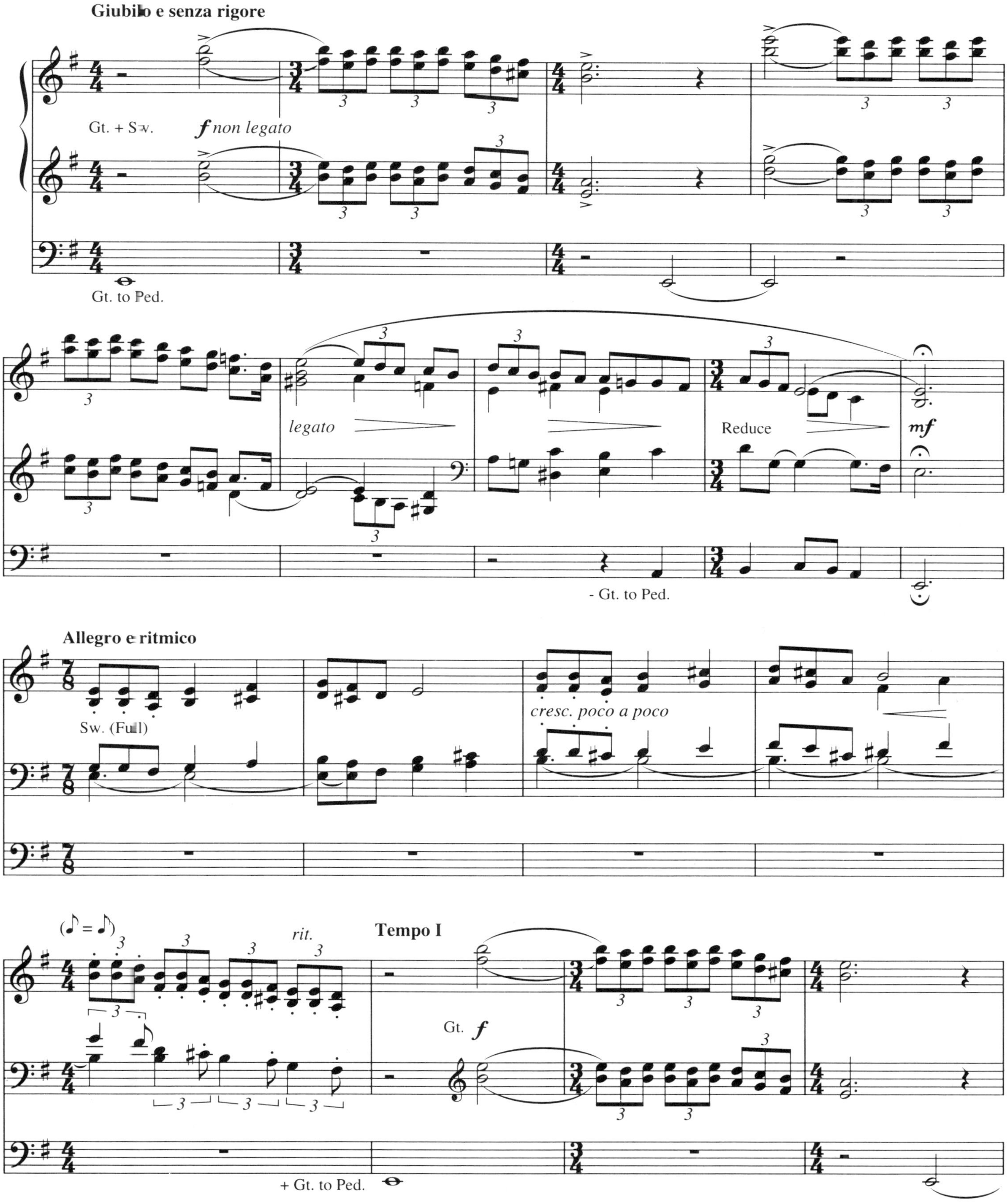

legato
Reduce
mf
(♩. = 52)
Ch. + Sw.
(- Reeds)
mf
poco rit.
Sw.
a tempo
mp
molto rit.

125

CHRISTUS PASTOR REX

Rosalie Bonighton

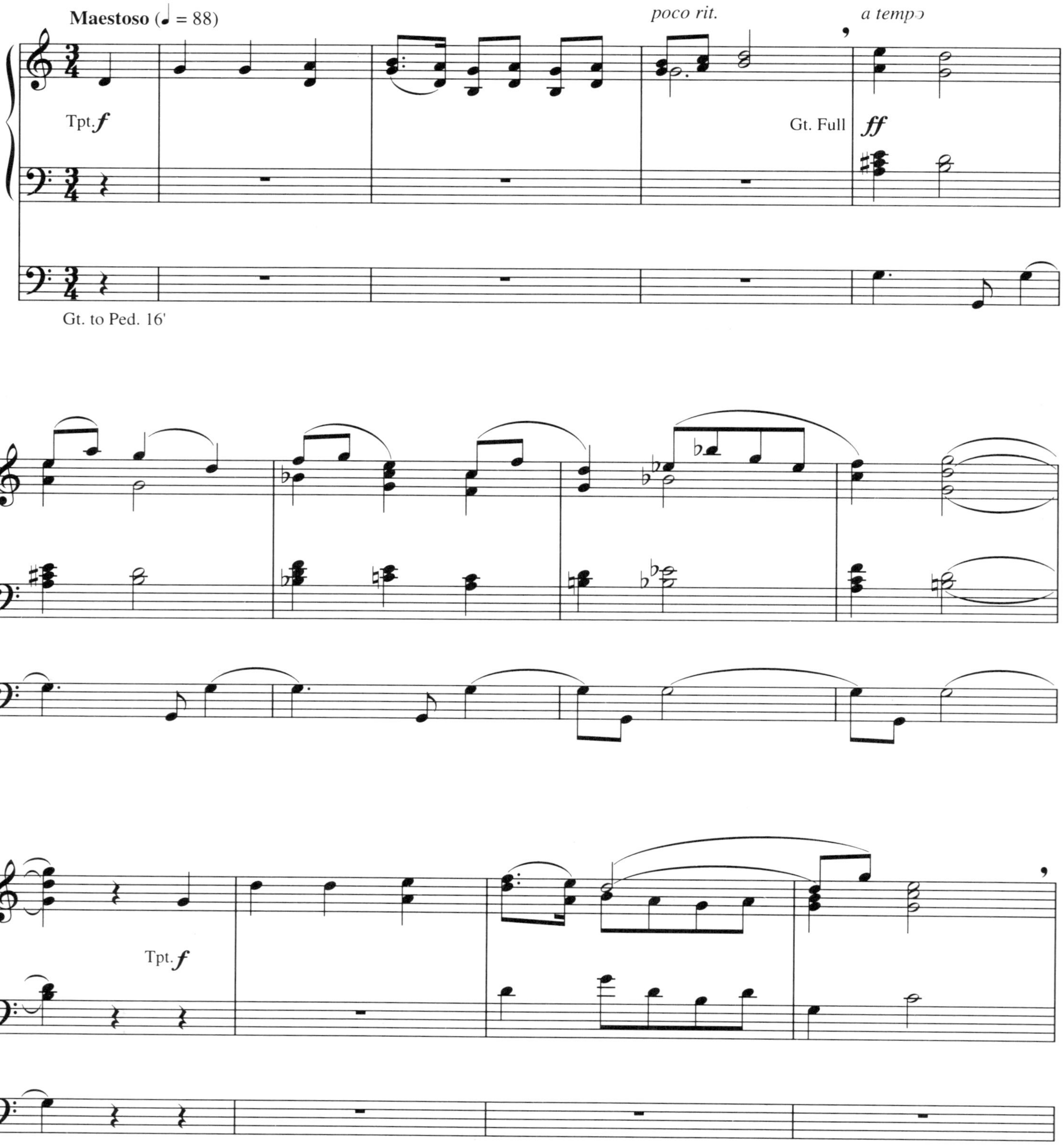

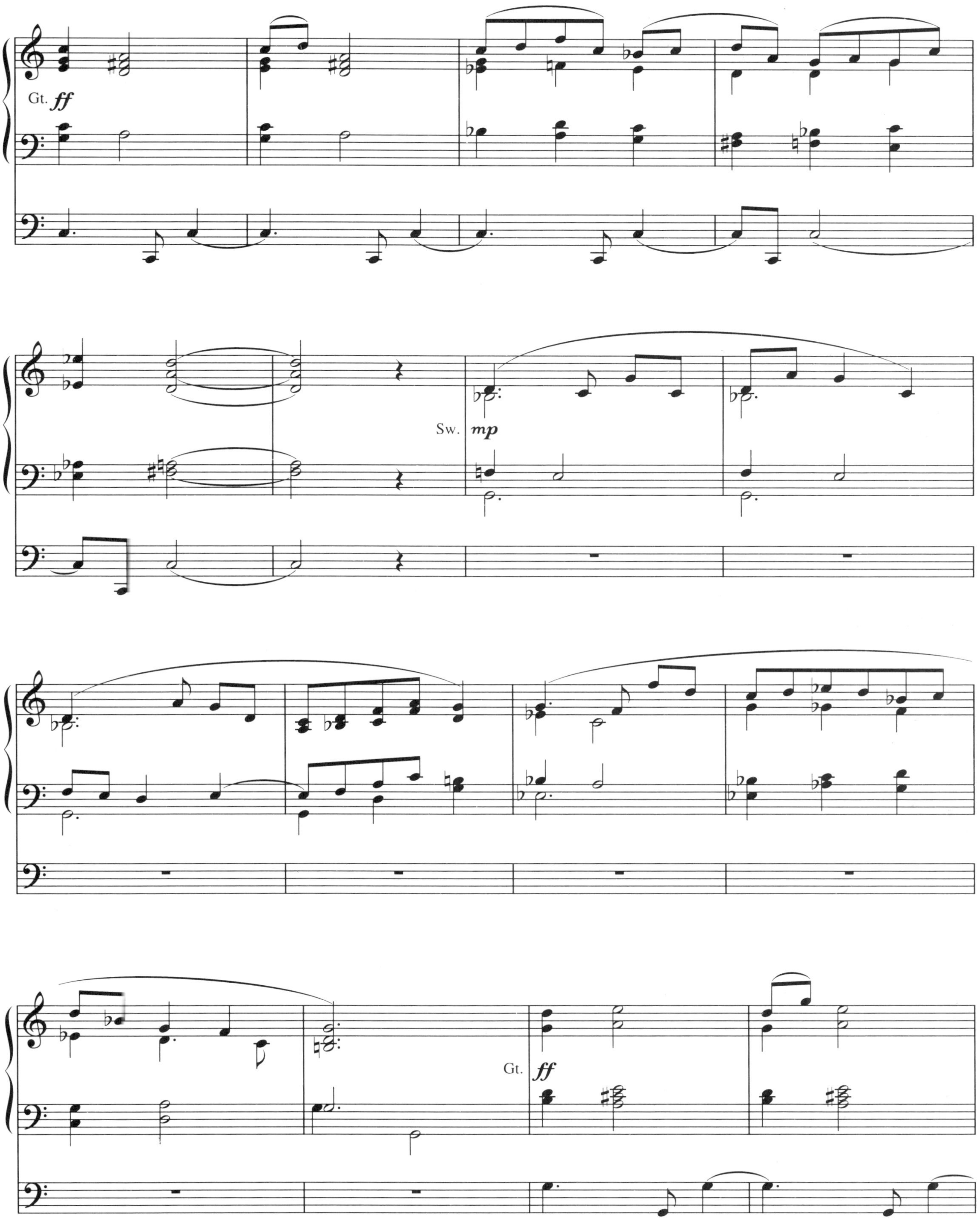
Gt. ff
Sw. mp
Gt. ff

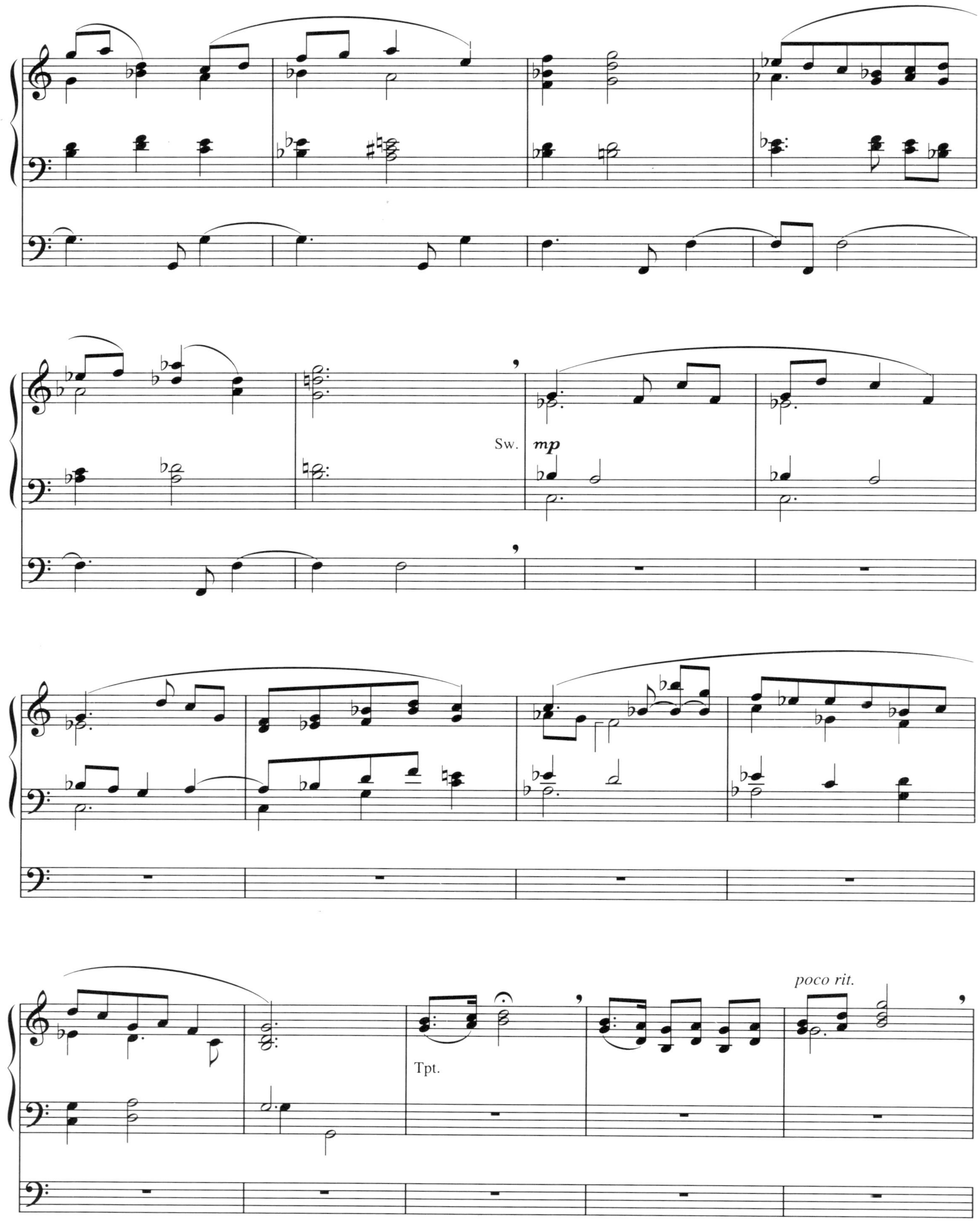

Sw.
mp
Tpt.
poco rit.

a tempo
Gt. ff
poco rit.
Tpt.
a tempo
Sw. mp
poco rit.
a tempo
rall.
Gt. + Tpt.
ff

SUNDAYS OF THE YEAR

Richard Pantcheff

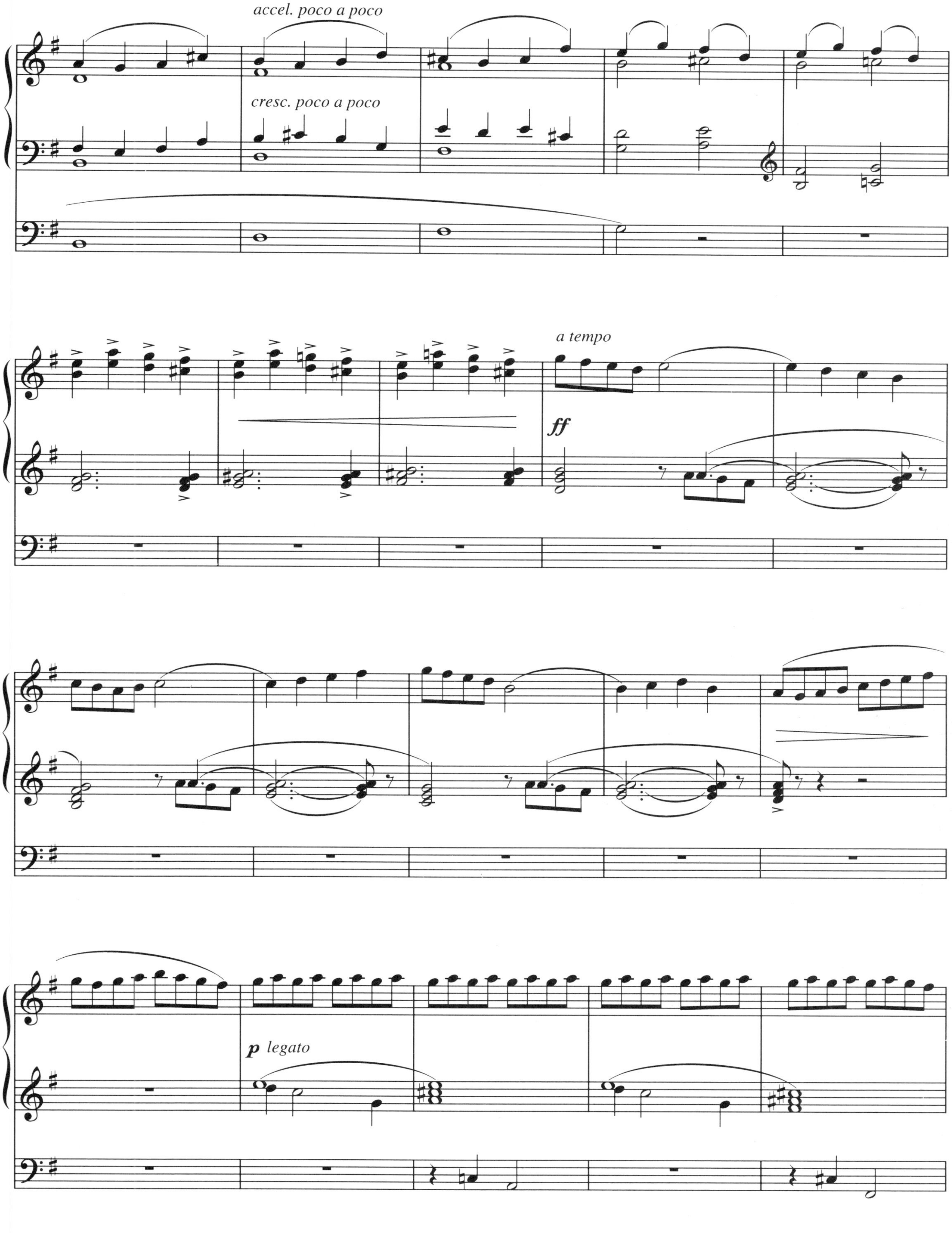
accel. poco a poco
cresc. poco a poco
a tempo
ff
p legato

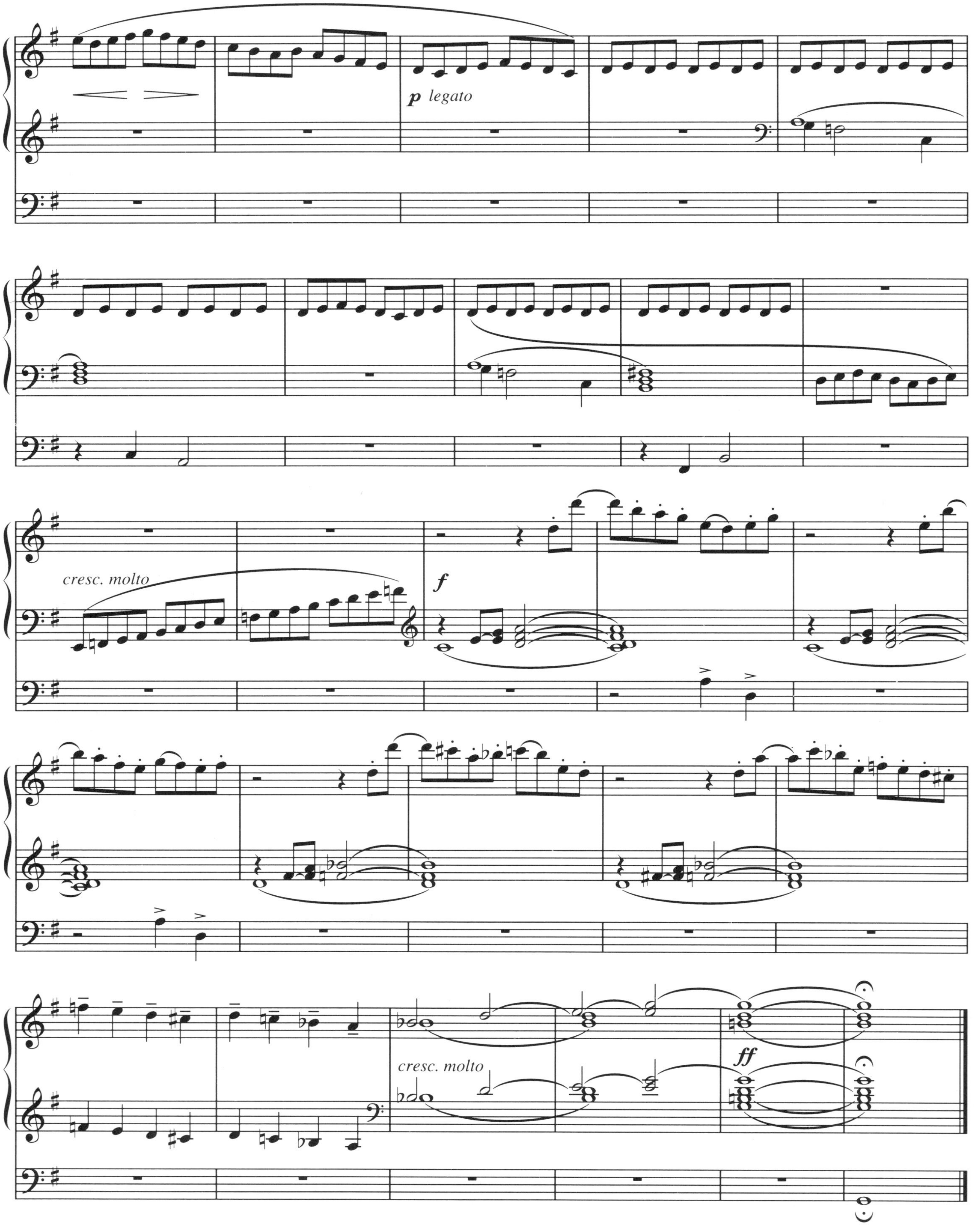
p legato
cresc. molto
f
cresc. molto
ff

QUONIAM TU SOLUS SANCTUS

Adrian Vernon Fish

133

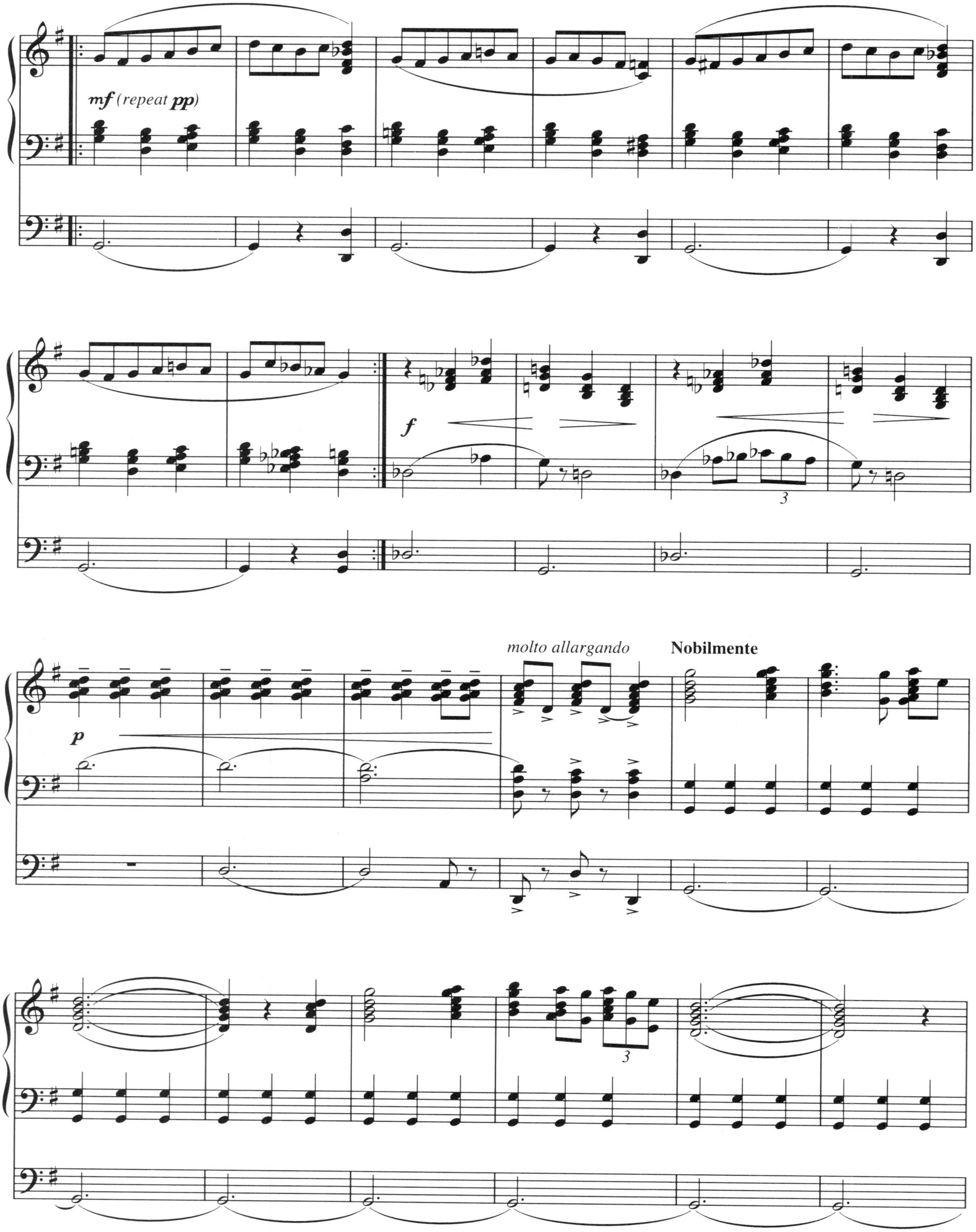
mf (repeat pp)
f
3
p
molto allargando
Nobilmente
3

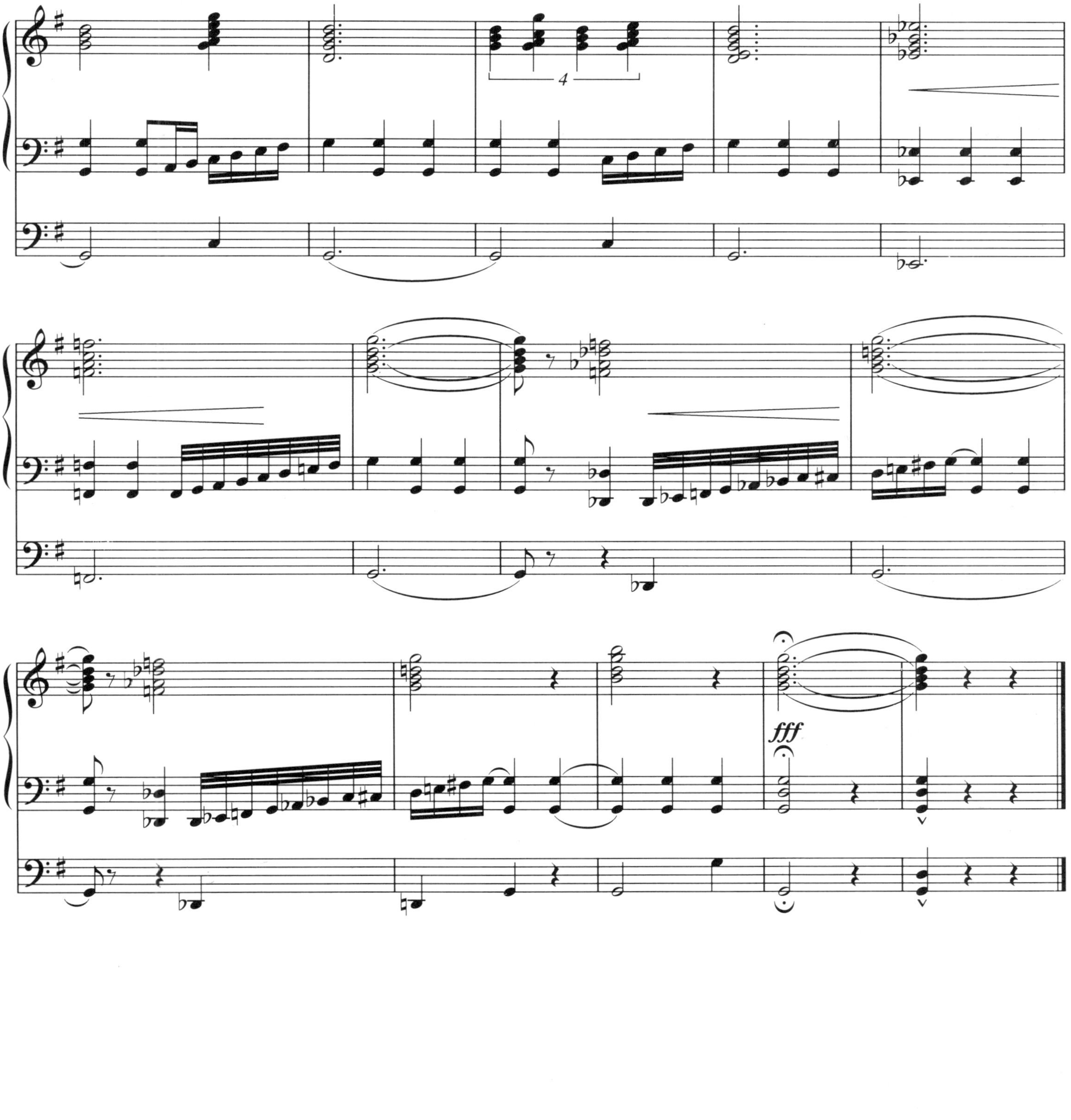
4
fff

ANDANTE CON MOTO

Christopher Tambling

poco rit.

⊕ CODA

rit.

D.C. al Coda

Fine

137

FEAST OF THE BLESSED VIRGIN

Malcolm McKelvey

Sw. Salicional, Celeste
Gt. Clarabella
Ch. Soft Reed
Ped. Soft 16' + Sw. to Ped.

Andante tranquillo

138

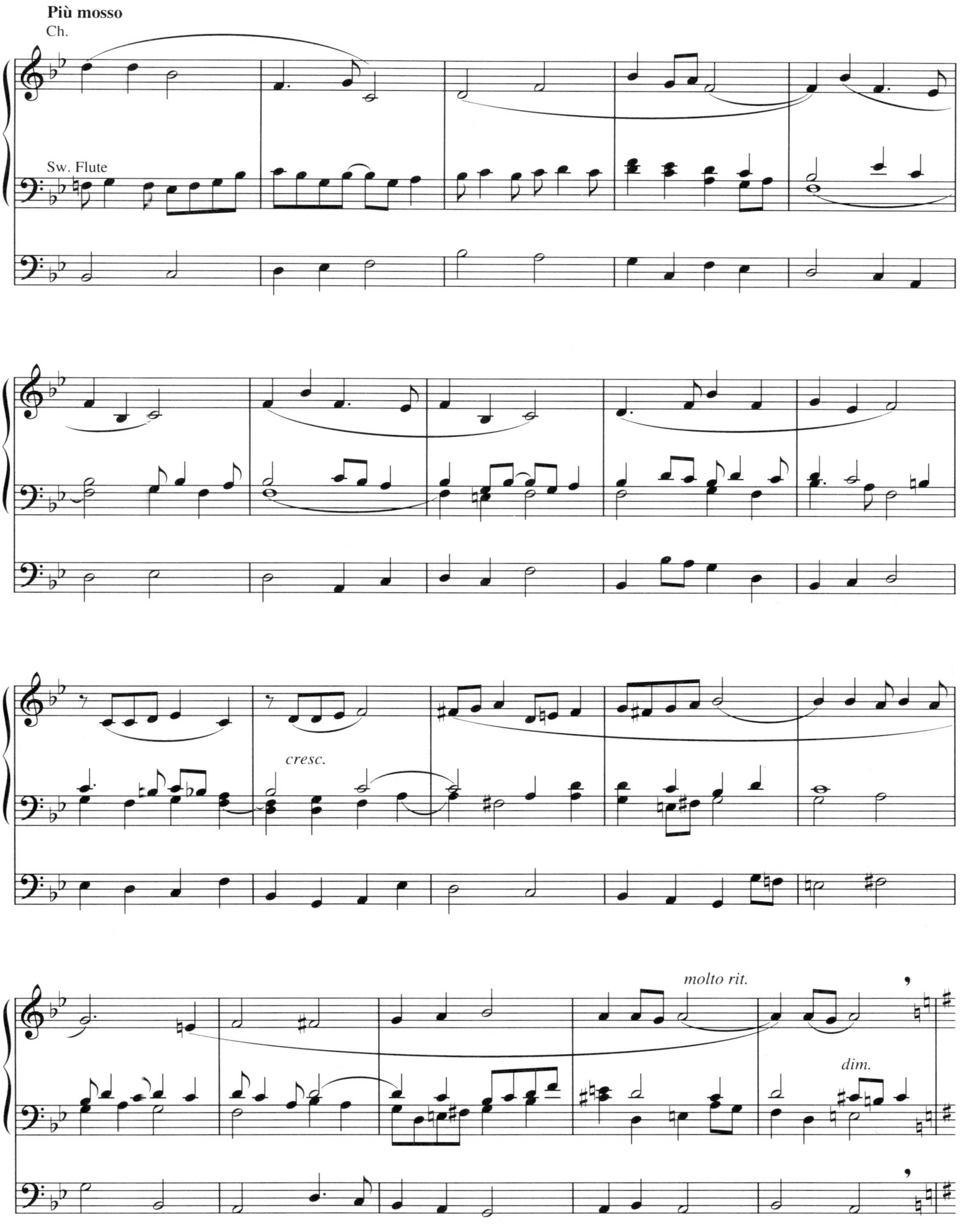
Più mosso
Ch.
Sw. Flute
cresc.
molto rit.
dim.

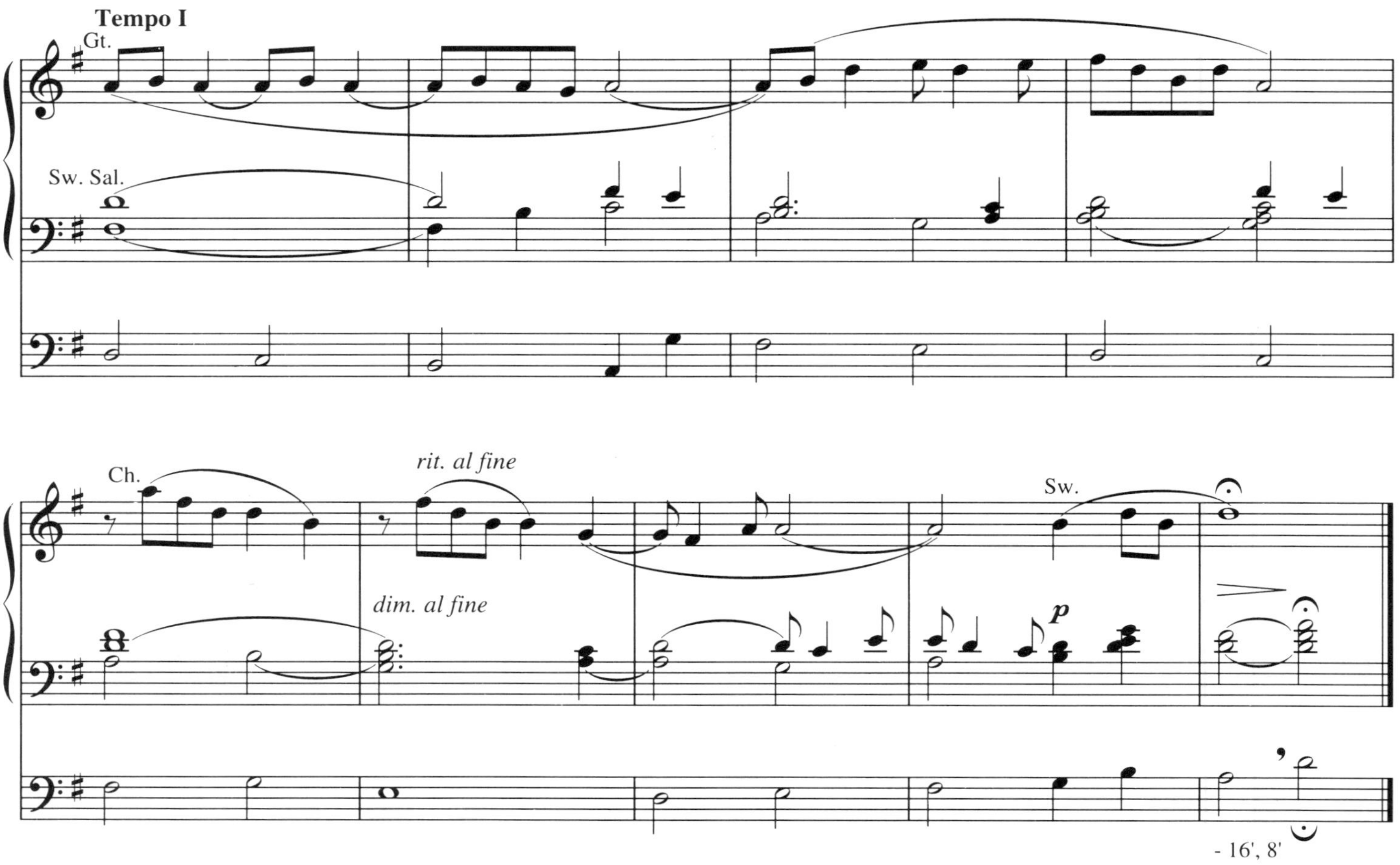
Tempo I
Gt.
Sw. Sal.
Ch.
rit. al fine
dim. al fine
Sw.
p
- 16', 8'

TOCCATA FOR HARVEST

Martin Setchell

Sw. 8', 4', (2')
Gt. 8' Trumpet
Ped. Soft 16'. 8', Sw. to Ped.

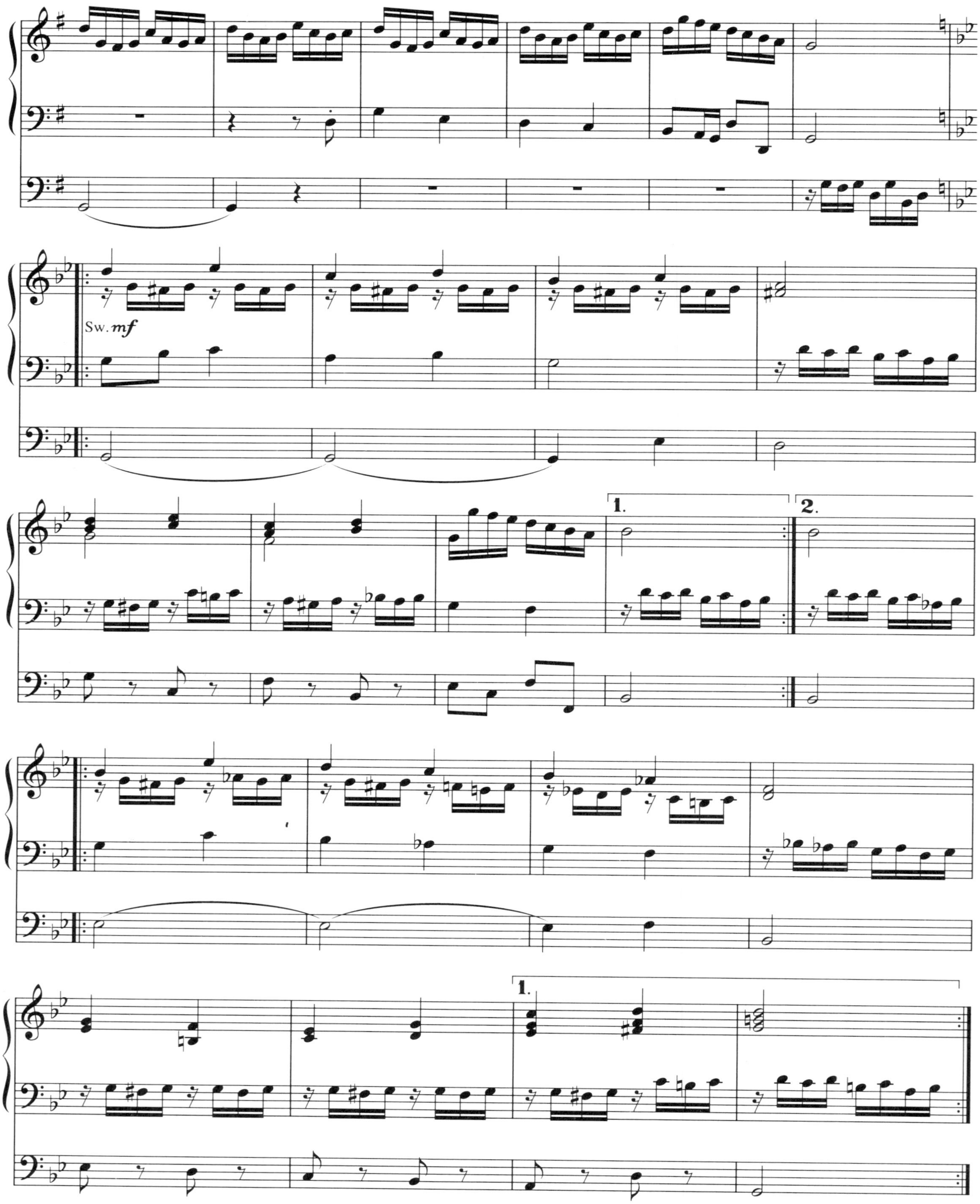
Sw. mf
1.
2.
1.

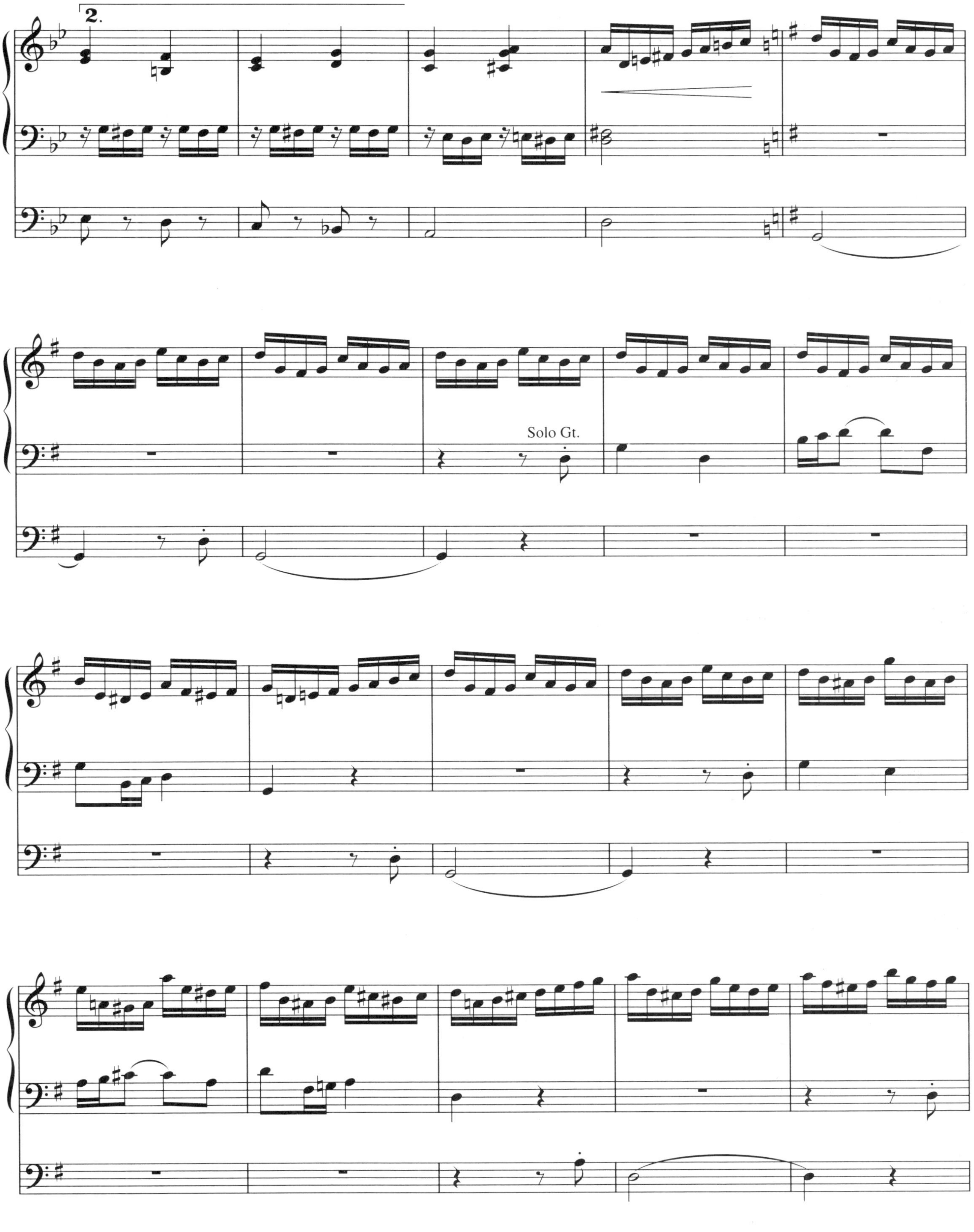
2.
Solo Gt.

+ Gt. (Full) to Ped. + Sw. to Gt.

Gt. (Sw. coupled) **ff**

fff

molto rit.

AVE MARIS STELLA

Colin Mawby

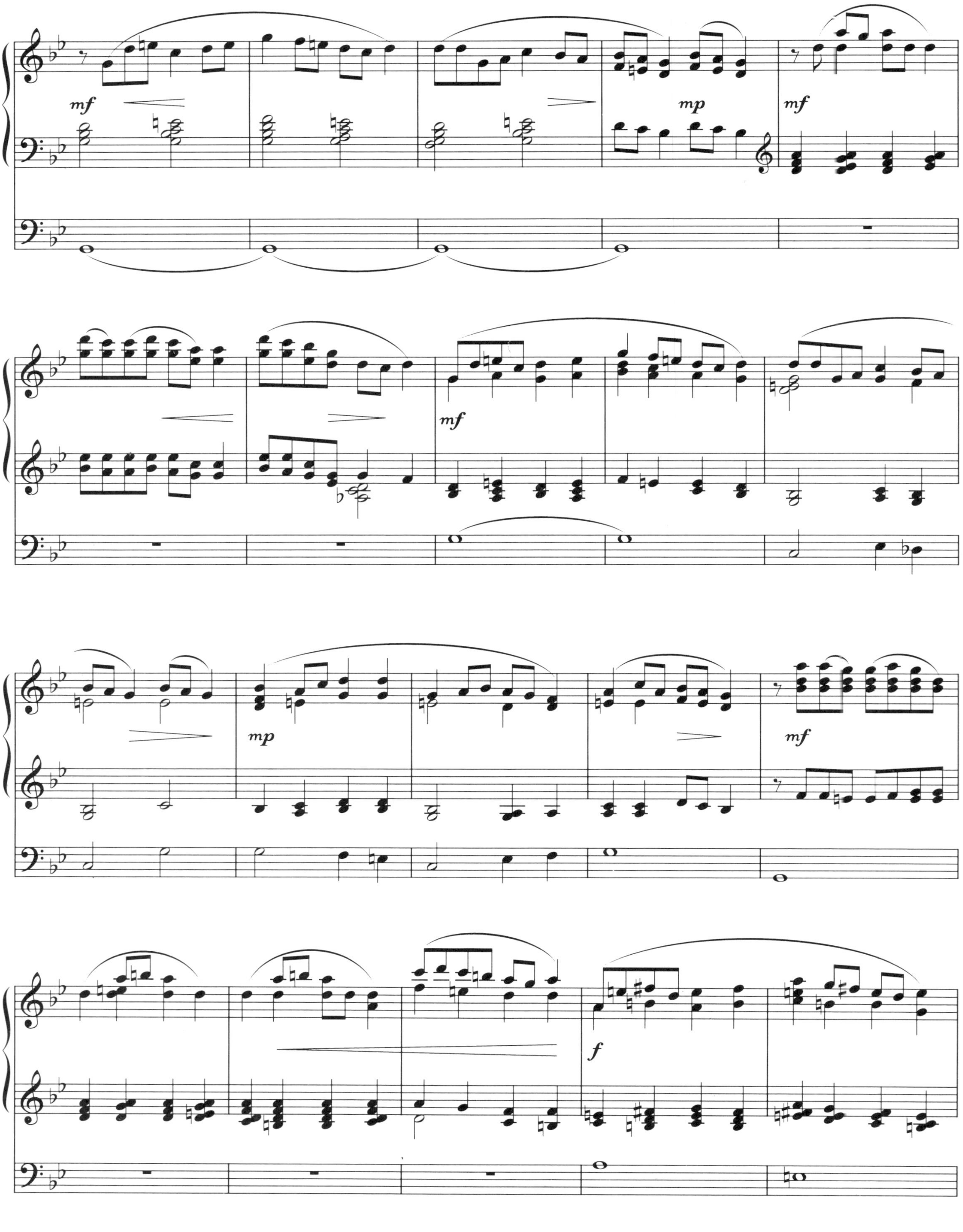
mf
mp
mf
mf
mp
mf
f

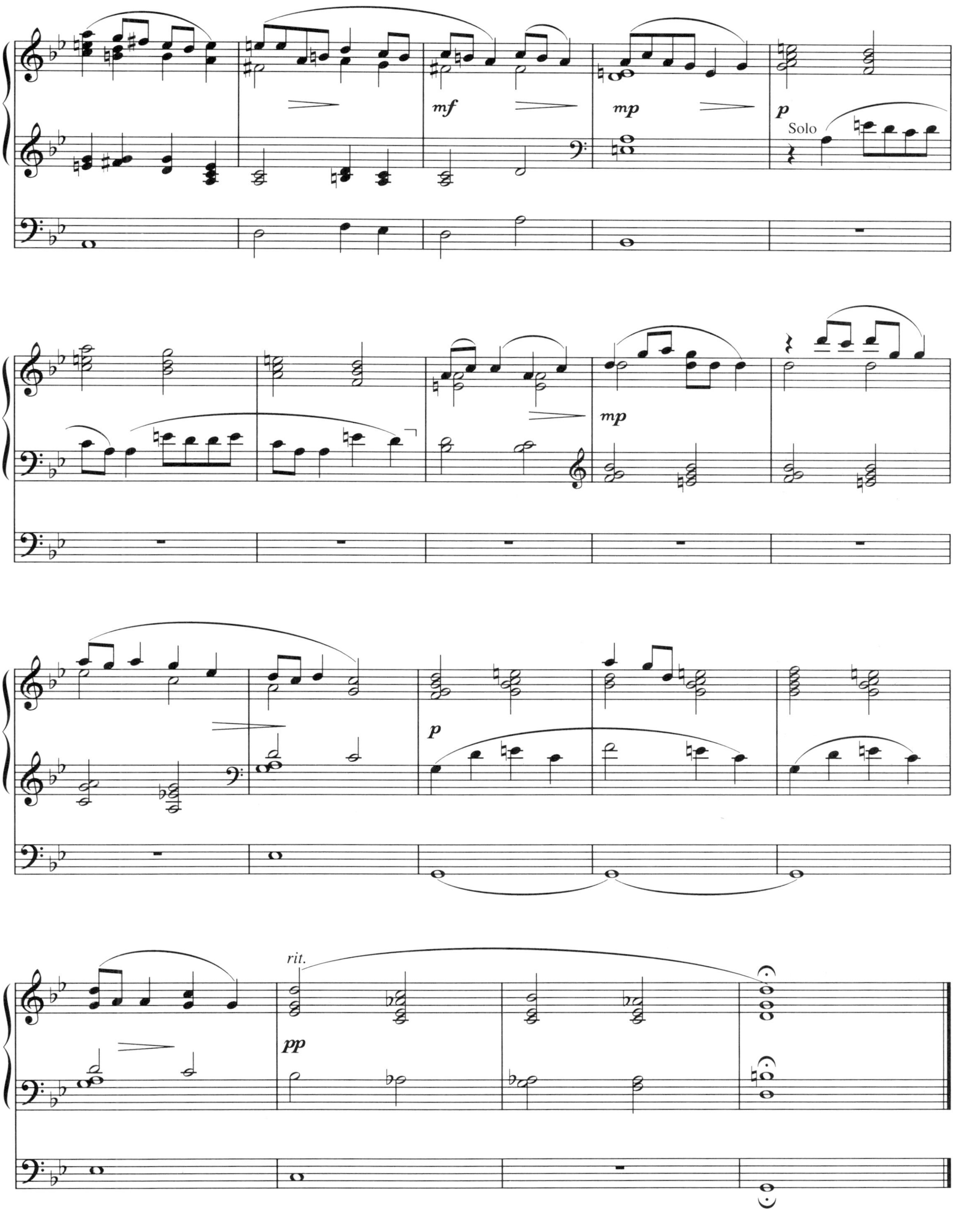
mf
mp
p
Solo
mp
p
rit.
pp

GAVOTTE AND JIG

Haymakers' Dance

Betty Roe

JIG

Fast and lightly

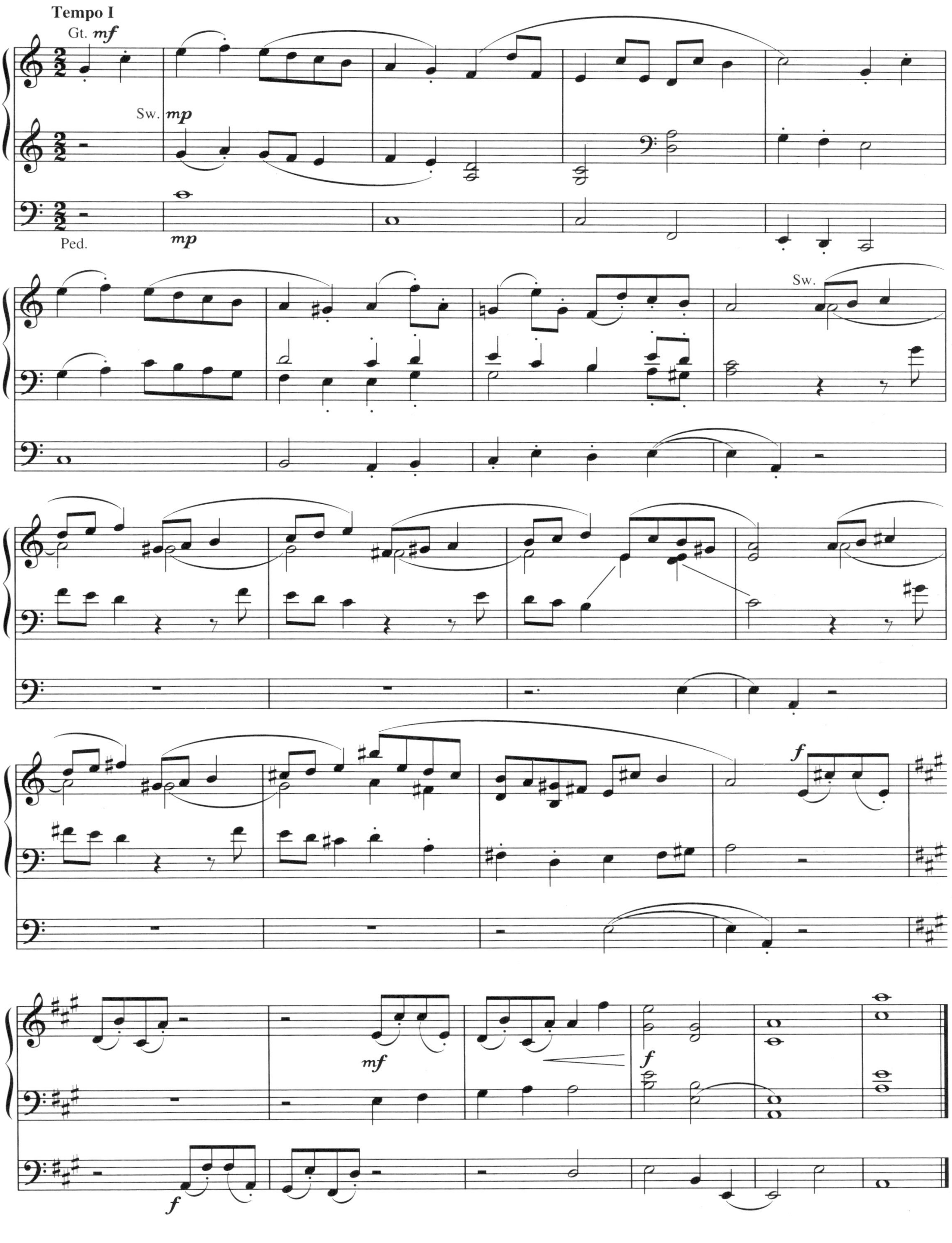
Tempo I
Gt. mf
Sw. mp
Ped.
mp
Sw.
f
mf
f
f

AVE MARIS STELLA

Andrew Moore

Based on the plainsong

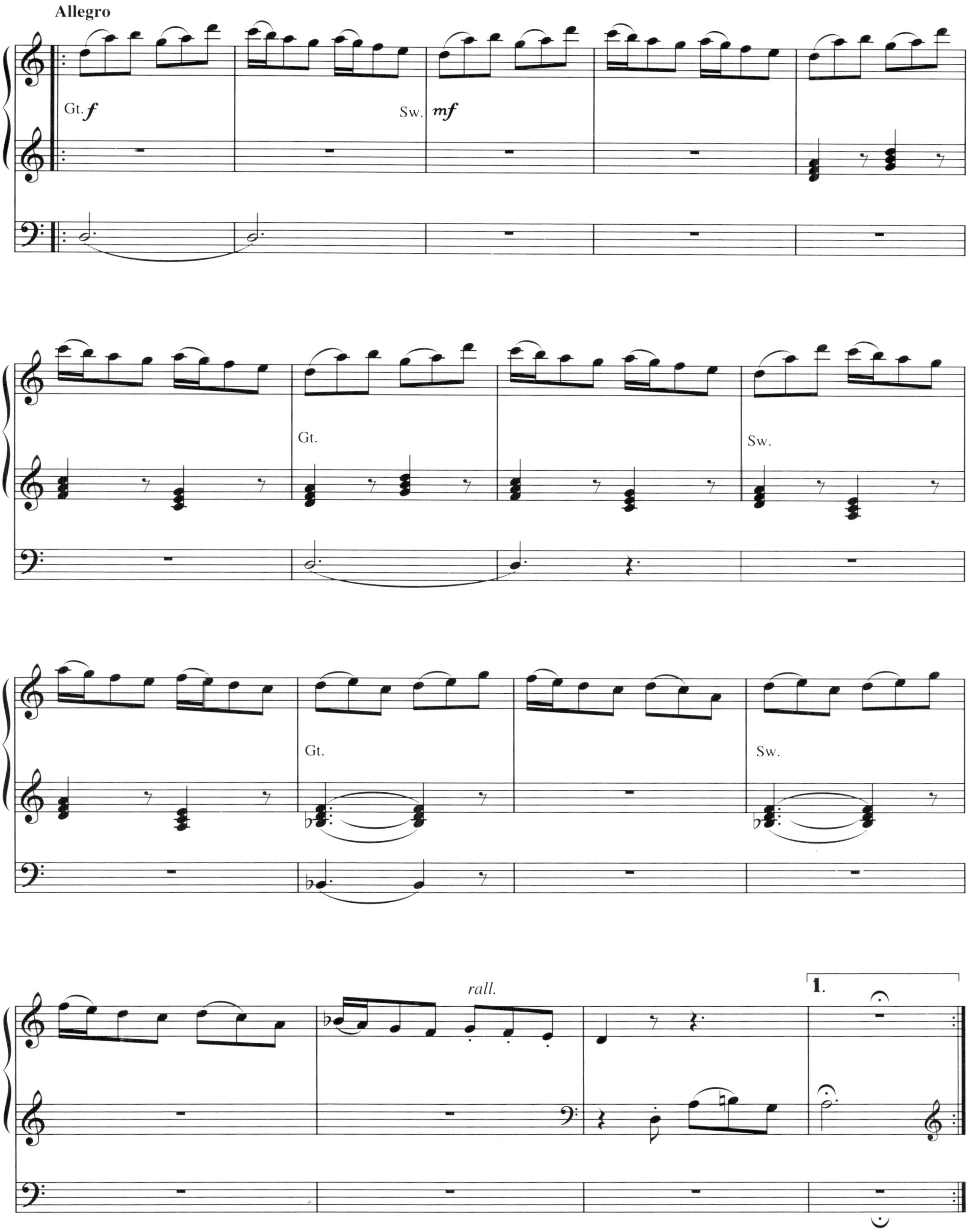

Allegro
Gt. f
Sw. mf
Gt.
Sw.
Gt.
Sw.
rall.
1.

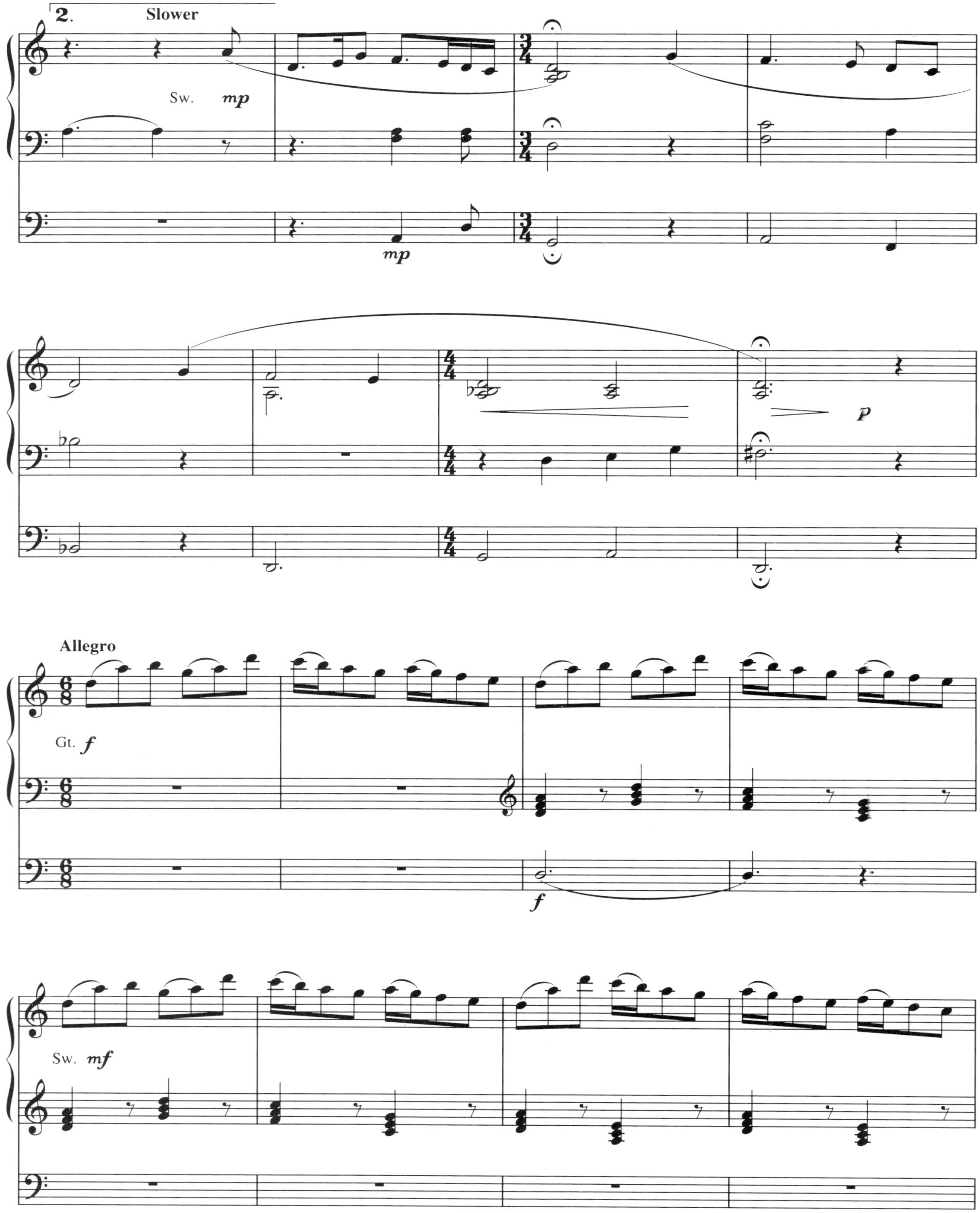
2.
Slower
Sw. mp
mp
p
Allegro
Gt. f
f
Sw. mf

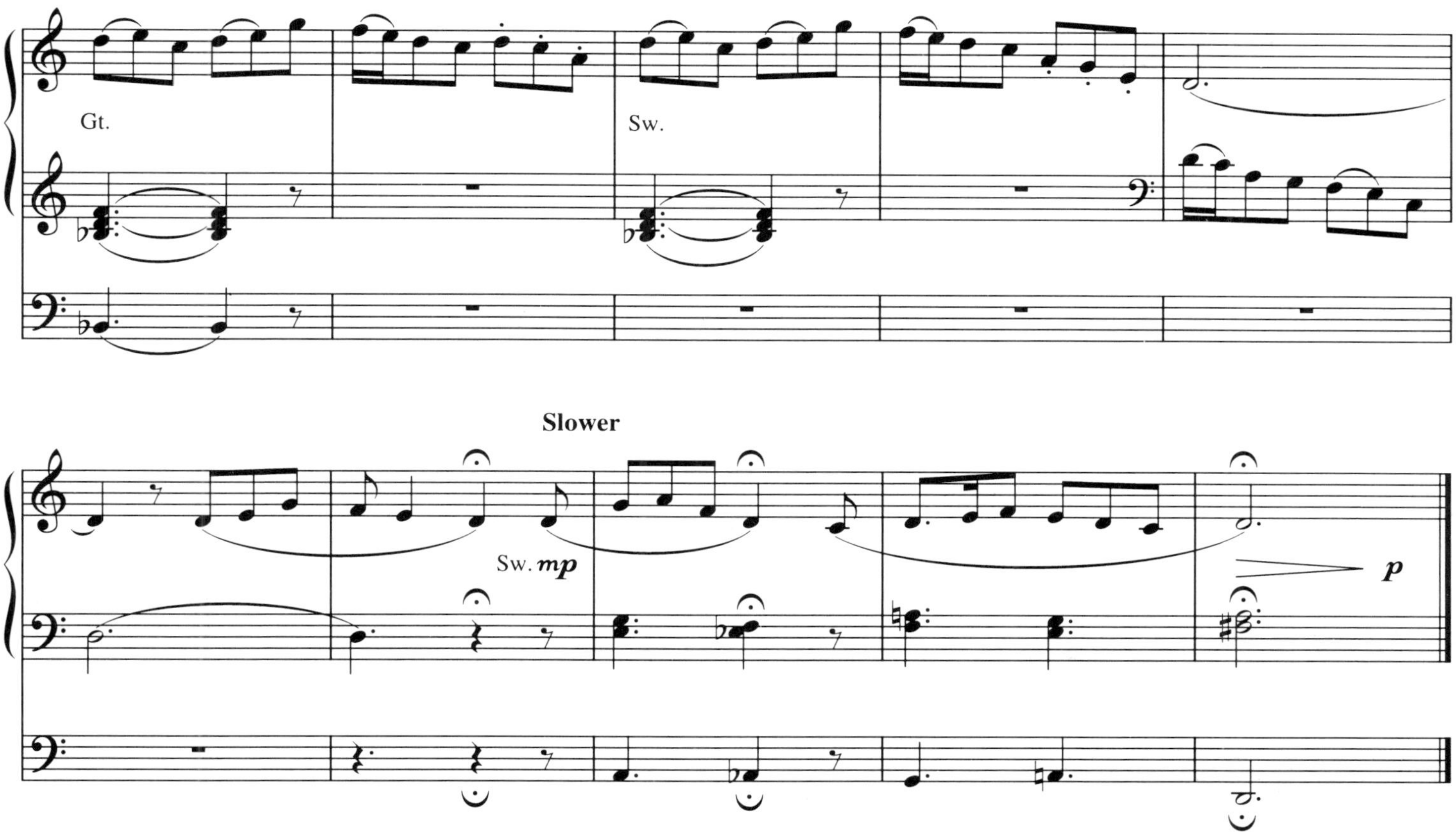
Gt.
Sw.
Slower
Sw. mp
p

VARIATIONS ON A FRENCH FOLK TUNE

June Nixon

Theme

Moderato e semplice (♩ = 96)

Variation I

Animato (♩ = 118)

Ch. 8' + 4'
(+ Sw.)

(Sw.)

(Gt.)   (Ch.)   (Sw.)

rall.

Variation II
L'istesso tempo (♩ = 86)

Variation III
Seriosamente (♩ = 98)

Variation IV

Gioioso (♩. = 63)

Variation V

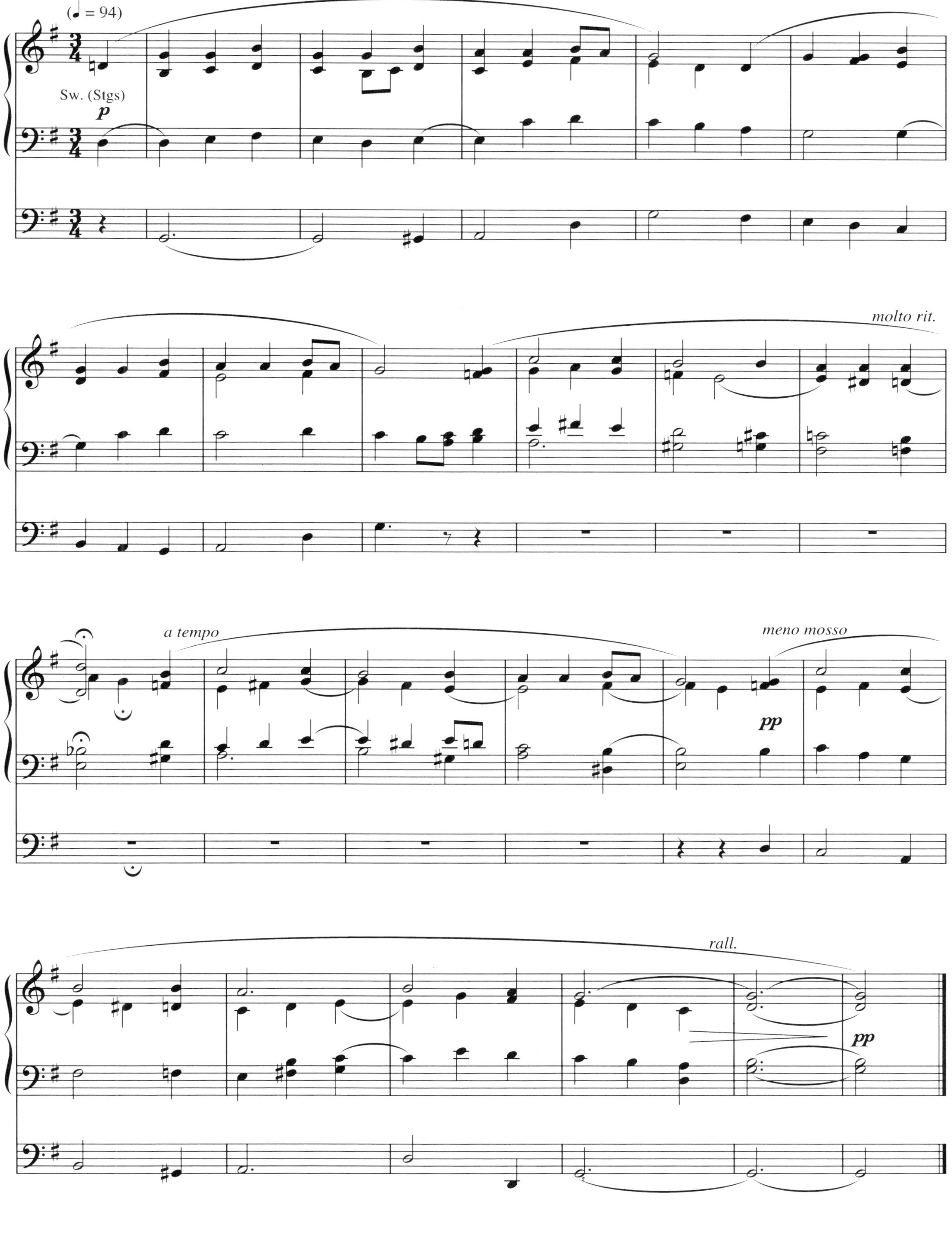

ELEGY

Richard Lloyd

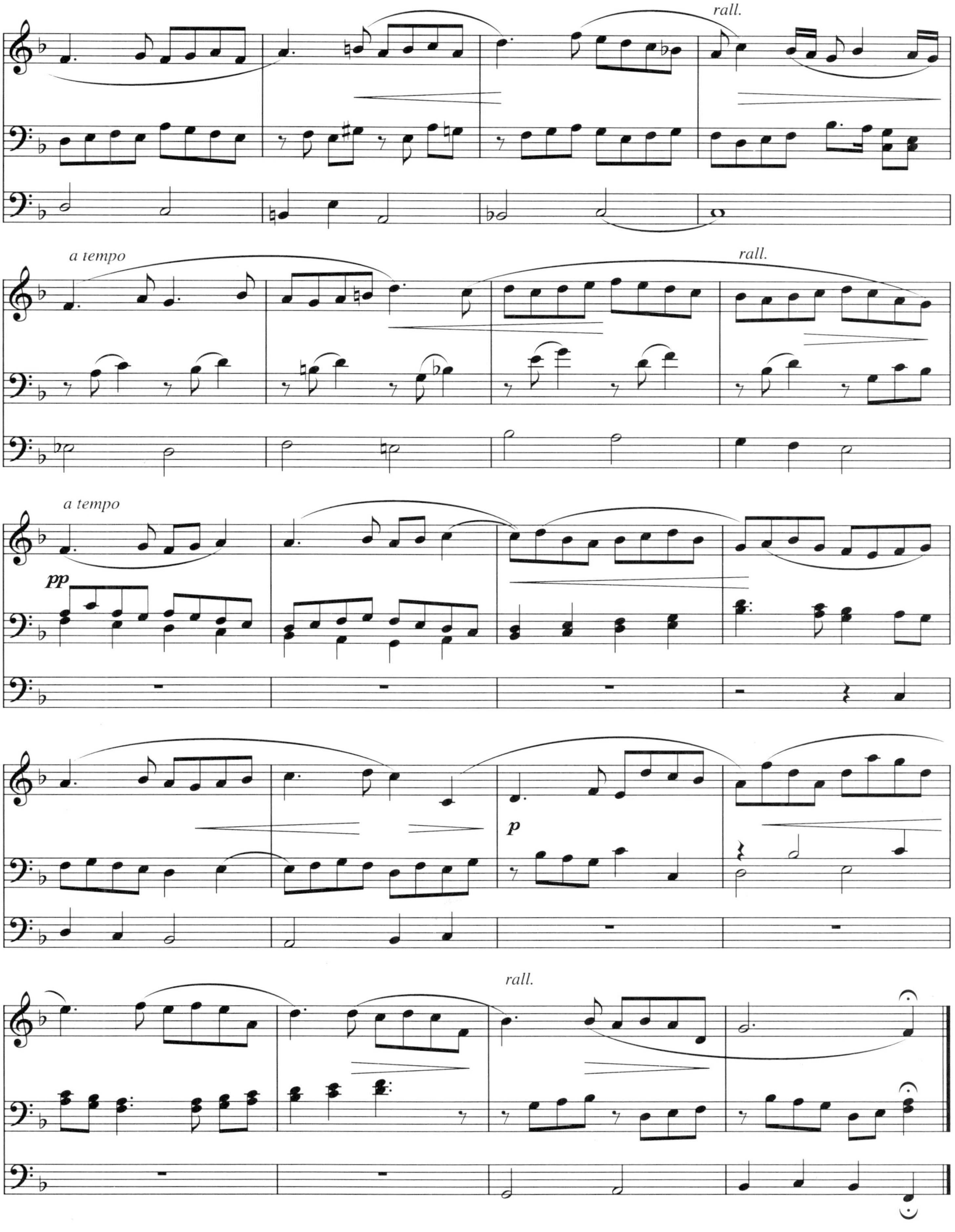
rall.
a tempo
rall.
a tempo
pp
p
rall.

REMEMBRANCE

Andrew Gant

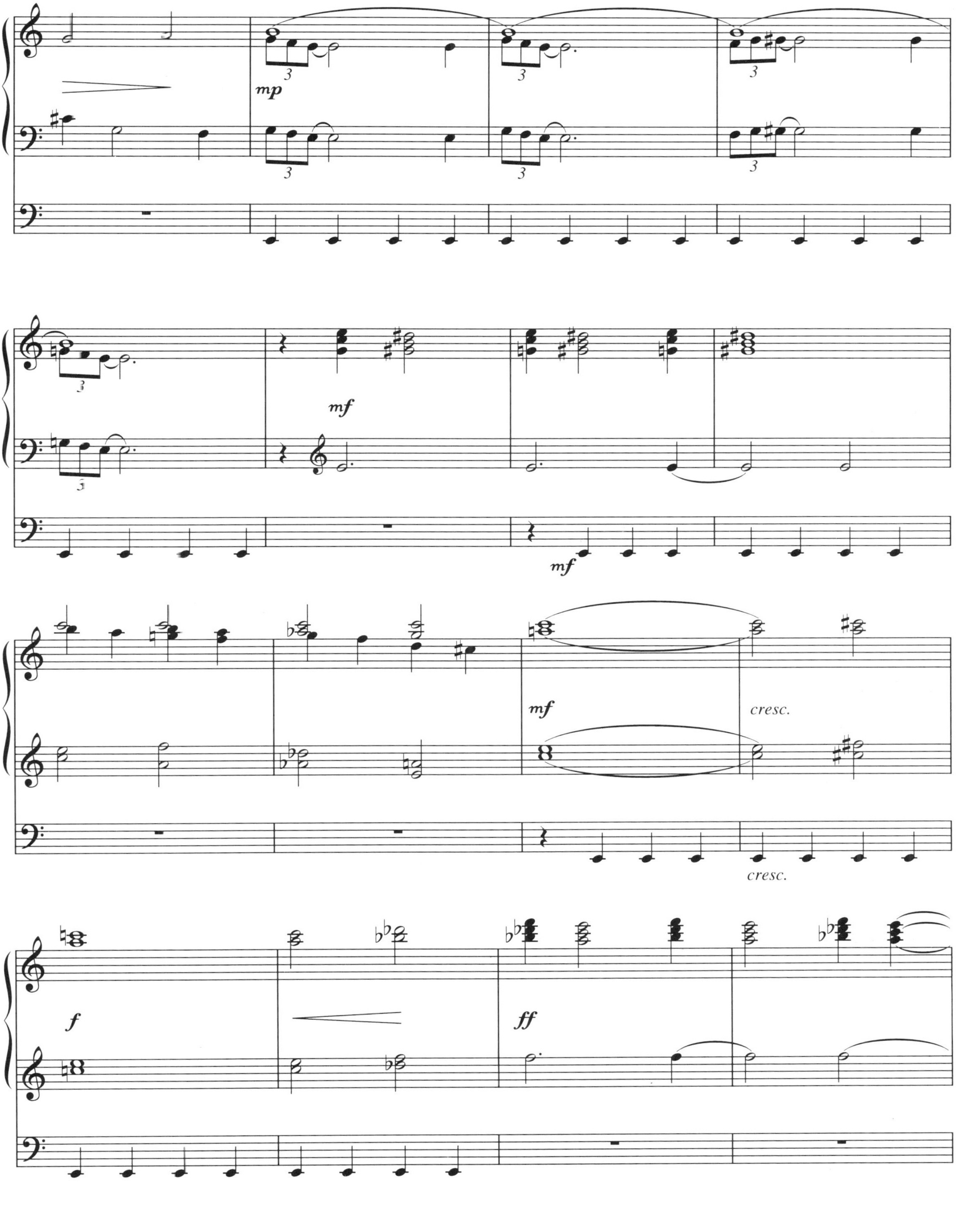

mp
mf
mf
mf
cresc.
cresc.
f
ff

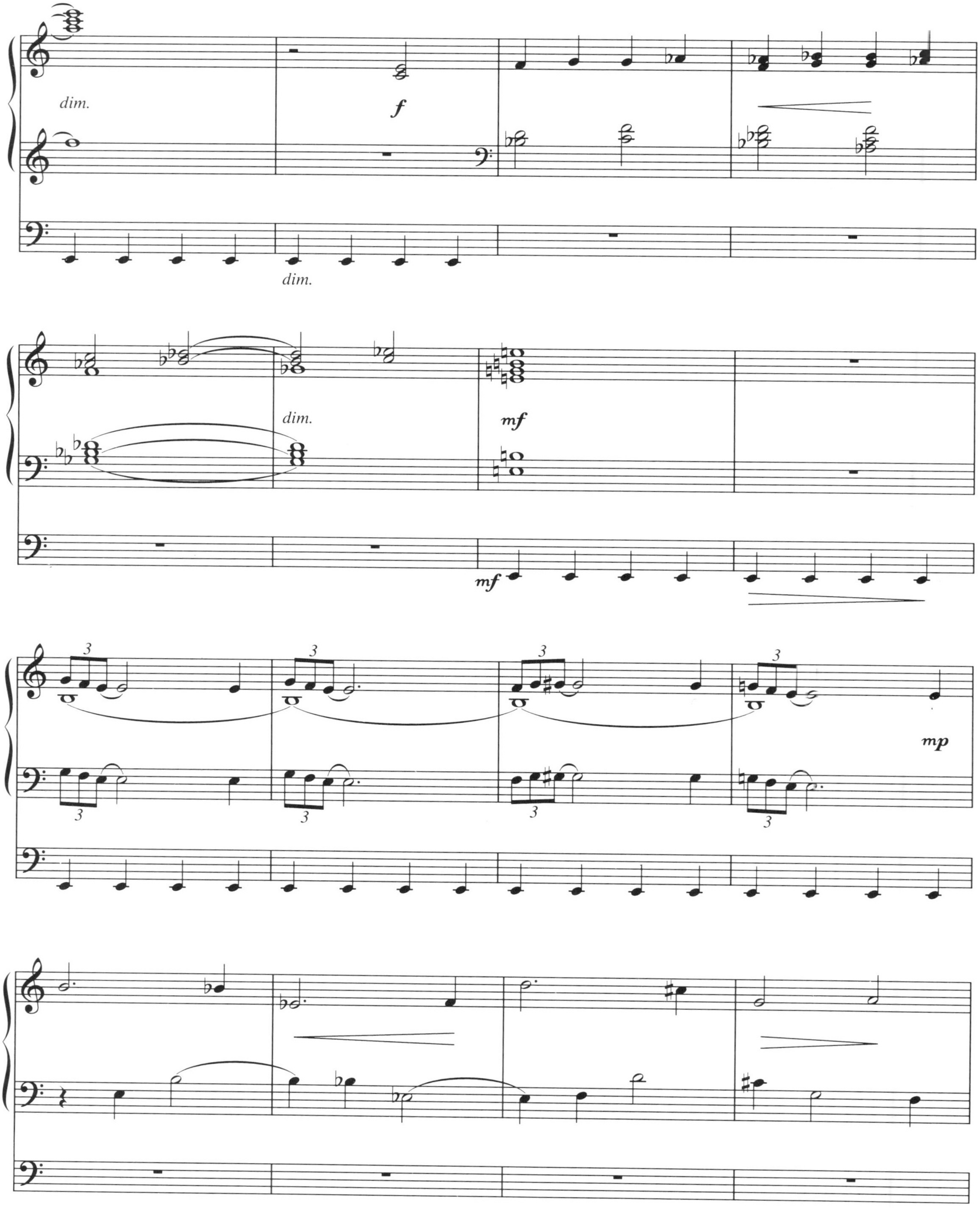
dim.
f
dim.
dim.
mf
mf
mp

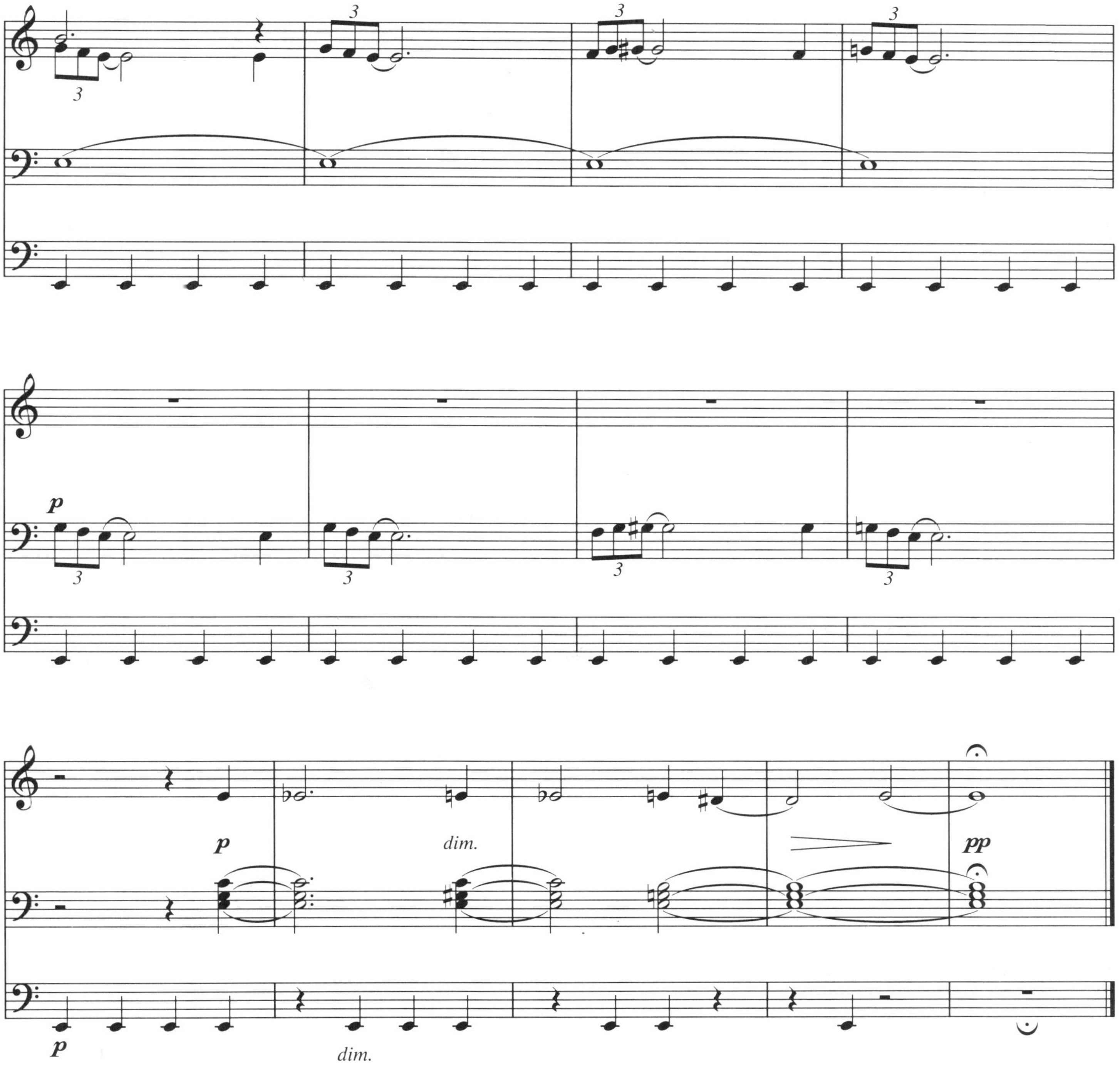
p
p
dim.
p
dim.
pp

About the Composers

Rosalie Bonighton (*b.*1946) is a recitalist, teacher and composer with a special interest in writing music for new liturgical needs.

Simon Clark (*b.*1975) has studied composition with many prominent English composers, including Howard Blake and Michael Finnissy. He is active in Sussex musical circles and takes a keen interest in the musical life of St Mary the Virgin Church, Hartfield.

Adrian Vernon Fish (*b.*1956) studied composition with Alan Ridout and Herbert Howells. His output is considerable, ranging from symphonies and organ music to cantatas and cabaret songs.

Andrew Fletcher (*b.*1950) is a teacher, composer, accompanist and recitalist, performing regularly all over the world.

Andrew Gant (*b.*1963) is Director of Music in Chapel at Selwyn College, Cambridge, and regularly tours with the choir, recently visiting Sweden, the USA and Italy. He is Organist and Master of the Choir at The Royal Military Chapel (The Guards' Chapel), Wellington Barracks, London, and teaches composition, harmony and counterpoint at the University of Cambridge.

Richard Lloyd (*b.*1933) was Assistant Organist of Salisbury Cathedral and successively Organist of Hereford and Durham Cathedrals. He now divides his time between examining and composing.

John Marsh (*b.*1939) formerly Organist and Director of Music at St Mary Redcliffe Church, Bristol, is now a member of the music staff at Clifton College, Bristol.

Colin Mawby (*b.*1936) was previously Choral Director at Radio Telefís Éireann, the national broadcasting authority in the Republic of Ireland, and Master of the Music at Westminster Cathedral. He is Conductor of Ireland's only full-time professional choir, the National Chamber Choir of Ireland.

Malcolm McKelvey (*b.*1926) was Organ Scholar at St Peter's College, Oxford. He was Director of Music at Christ's Hospital in Horsham, Sussex (the Bluecoat School), for 23 years prior to his retirement in 1985.

Andrew Moore (*b.*1954) is parish priest of Lambourn and Hungerford.

June Nixon is Organist and Director of the Choir at St Paul's Cathedral, Melbourne, Australia. She also teaches at the Melbourne University School of Music.

Richard Pantcheff (*b.*1959) is an organist and composer currently working in Oxford. Many of his works are written for the Episcopal Church of Christ the King, Frankfurt, Germany, as Composer in Association.

James Patten (*b.*1936) is a composer and conductor who has held a variety of lecturing posts at Universities and Colleges, including Professor of Composition at Trinity College of Music.

Richard Proulx (*b.*1937) is a composer, conductor and organist. He was Music Director at the Cathedral of the Holy Name in Chicago for fourteen years. His ensemble 'The Cathedral Singers' is well known for its series of recordings of both early music and original works.

Betty Roe (*b.*1930) studied at the Royal Academy of Music and later with Lennox Berkeley. She composes in a variety of forms – from solo songs to operas.

Martin Setchell (*b.*1949) is an English-born and trained musician, choral conductor and organ recitalist now working in New Zealand, where he is Senior Lecturer in Music at the University of Christchurch and Organist at the Christchurch Town Hall.

Christopher Tambling (*b.*1964) is Director of Music at Downside School and Master of the Schola Cantorum of Downside Abbey. He was previously Director of Music at Glenalmond College and Perth City Organist. He received his musical training at Christ's Hospital as a pupil of Malcolm McKelvey, and was Organ Scholar of St Peter's College, Oxford. He is a Fellow of the Royal College of Organists.

Stanley Vann (*b.*1910) was successively Organist at Chelmsford and Peterborough Cathedrals.